BY THE SAME AUTHOR

Poetry

Reading Geographies

Road Into Autumn

A Change of Season

Matelot

Criticism

The Poetry of Robert Graves

W.H. Davies: Man and Poet

THE POETRY OF HAROLD MONRO

THE POETRY
OF HAROLD MONRO

MICHAEL CULLUP

Greenwich Exchange
London

Greenwich Exchange, London

First published in Great Britain in 2018
All rights reserved

The Poetry of Harold Monro
© Michael Cullup, 2018

This book is sold subject to the conditions that it shall not, by way of trade or otherwise, be lent, resold, hired out or otherwise circulated without the publisher's prior consent in any form of binding or cover other than that in which it is published and without a similar condition including this condition being imposed on the subsequent purchaser.

Printed and bound by imprintdigital.com
Cover design by December Publications
Tel: 07951511275

Greenwich Exchange Website: www.greenex.co.uk

Cataloguing in Publication Data is available
from the British Library

ISBN: 978-1-910996-25-6

CONTENTS

1 The Right Thing *9*

2 Restlessness *18*

3 Theory and Practice *25*

4 Alida Monro *30*

5 The Poetry Bookshop *38*

6 The Poems *46*

   A Selection of Poems *57*

   Bibliography

1
THE RIGHT THING

Harold Monro seems almost completely forgotten today, yet he was at one time a well-known and much respected poet and publisher. Who would have thought that the editor of the very first number of *Poetry Review*, and the creator and editor of the very influential *Poetry and Drama*, would fade from view himself, his poetry unread and his reputation as someone who was at the centre of a revolutionary change in literary history (as well as contributing to the success of poets who now have a secure place in the English poetic tradition) would himself become of no apparent significance? And who, now, recalls the fact that Monro ran the very successful Poetry Bookshop in London? There was hardly a poet of any importance at the time who didn't either buy poetry books from him or read at the poetry readings he organised.

But, perhaps, the fact that he was so closely associated with the so-called 'Georgian' poets has damaged his reputation to such an extent that his poems have been relegated to that now disparaged transitory fashion in British literary history: a history crowded with literary fashions and factions of one kind and another. Yet, it needs to be remembered that his poetry was much valued by T.S. Eliot, who not only published him, but also said that 'his poetry, as a whole, is more nearly the right thing than any of the poetry of a somewhat older generation than mine except Mr Yeats.' Whatever we might think of Yeats (and he certainly seems to have established a secure place in our literary history) Eliot's approval is some accolade from a literary figure as important as Yeats in the history of twentieth-century poetry. And not only Eliot, but Ezra Pound too admired his work, although both poets were not uncritical of his deficiencies.

Of course, one must not get too carried away by the rise and fall of literary reputations. We all acquire our likes and dislikes from our private reading, although the influence of teachers, literary reviews, and the continuous pressures of the literary establishment sometimes distort our attempt to form a stable view of matters. You might have thought that poets were born with some kind of immunity to the swing of the literary pendulum but, sadly, this is not the case. Anyone with half an ear can identify the superficial difference between eighteenth-century poetry and the poetry of, say, the Victorians, and these obvious differences are reinforced by the almost automatic grouping of those poets who headed the fashion: Pope, Johnson, Goldsmith; Wordsworth, Keats, Coleridge; Tennyson, Browning, Arnold, and so on. And each major grouping accumulated around it a positive swarm of poetic imitators. Most of those who bother to read poetry become more or less accustomed to these major groupings, more or less accepting the judgements of their peers, whoever they might be.

At the same time, there is a certain amount of unease over the importance of those individuals who haunt the lesser slopes of Parnassus. From time to time, literary dictators of one kind or another (an Arnold, or a Leavis) tell us what's what. Indeed, Eliot, in his way, was quietly dictatorial, and Pound was noisily so.

These fashion-setters, whether poets or literary critics, give strength to the timid and boost the confidence of those who waver nervously on the fringes of decision. Unfortunately, readers do appear to like being told rather than finding out for themselves. There is always a queue for the opinions of those reviewers who have staked their claim to some special kind of literary discernment.

These literary tides are strong enough to frustrate even the strongest of swimmers. Emerging poets who tentatively put their foot into literary waters are discouraged by such a cold prospect and intimidated by the fury on the horizon. Of those who strike out into the waves, only the desperately ambitious have any real chance of recognition and success. And most readers of poetry are only interested in the obviously successful.

The resultant map is one of literary fashions, or periods, headed by what are known as 'major' figures. These major figures somehow become established over time and their reputations are rarely challenged. When an established reputation *is* challenged, it becomes something of a literary event. In the meantime, the positive swarm of minor figures increases year by year. But it is as well to remember that some of them are minor purely by accident, as it were. Monro, perhaps, is one of them.

Georgian poetry gets its name from the title of a series of five anthologies backed by the initiative and money of Edward Marsh who, at the age of forty, was Secretary to the First Lord of the Admiralty, Winston Churchill. He had become not only an important Civil Servant at a relatively young age but also someone who moved in influential circles, with a refined interest in the Arts, especially poetry. He was a close friend of one of the leading poets in what became the Georgian movement: Rupert Brooke. *Georgian Poetry*, financed by Marsh, whose own taste in poetry was predominantly responsible for the content of the anthologies, became identified with all those negatives a future generation of literary mages scornfully referred to as 'Georgian Poetry'. And Monro, its publisher, whose own poems found a secure place in its pages, has become tarred with the same brush.

It's essential to accept the fact that literary judgements about what is major and what is minor are not cast in stone. Robert Graves used to say something to the effect that every poet is in a minority of one. So, indeed, are poetry readers, provided that they are prepared to exercise their own judgement and trust their own taste. There is no doubt that this is never easy, simply because of the constant pressure towards conformity and homogeneity. But the vitality of literature (in this case, poetry) depends on it. Georgian poetry isn't bad poetry. Most of the poets who are placed within that category possessed great gifts, but those gifts were sacrificed on the altar of a particular fashion. Fashions change. In the case of poetry, ruthlessly. And fashions carry with them a great tide of poets, reviewers, and readers. In what sense Georgian poetry was deficient was defined by those poets who were determined to reform the tastes of a generation. Their success inevitably destroyed the reputations of their forebears.

Monro was in the thick of all this. He was an editor, a publisher, the manager of a thriving poetry bookshop and, dangerously so, a poet. He knew all the prominent poets of his time, he read and wrote in the maelstrom of a literary turmoil which threatened to overwhelm whatever talent he had. He followed, with contradiction after contradiction, the turn of poetic events, unable to decide how or what he was going to write. He knew too much, and he knew too many people. He was generous to the point of self-destruction. Yet, in the midst of all this confusion, he struggled to write his own kind of poetry.

Eliot was quick to point out that Monro 'was not an innovator' as far as poetic technique is concerned but that he had 'little in common' with Georgian poetry. He had a poetic personality and manner of writing which was not wholly in tune with the much anthologised verse of his day. However, Eliot strongly felt that the real difference between Monro and his fellow Georgians could be experienced only by reading his poems as a whole and sensing the continuous development towards increasing depth and the capacity to express his own personal suffering as he tried to make sense of his life.

According to Eliot, Monro's development brought him close to the manner of 'his younger contemporaries', meaning those poets who were striving to confront intellectual and emotional issues in a reinvigorated and more challenging poetic style. And, of course, Eliot himself was one of them. He was one of those who thought that things needed to be said which late nineteenth-century poetic conventions could not accommodate. To Eliot, Monro was a 'tortured' spirit, striving to express his own mental and emotional suffering 'faithfully' and without conventional restriction. In that sense, his work would retain its integrity as long as his poems were read, and read in the right kind of way. In Eliot's view, Monro, unlike many of his contemporaries, was a poet whose imaginative life was stimulated more by the city than by the country. His 'country' poems were those of someone whose interest in such matters was temporary and superficial and, though he wrote poems about the country, they were poems by a man who, in Eliot's words, 'would flee to the country' although 'his country (was) that of the man who must tomorrow return to town'.

Although his practical achievements would seem to contradict the idea, Monro was an intensely introverted character: his 'ceaseless question and answer', his disturbing dreams, his struggle to engage with the personal and the subjective and with the emotional burden of dealing with, and understanding, his own relationships were constant preoccupations. Nothing, for Monro, was ever easy. He was continuously reviewing and evaluating his own mental responses to being alive yet burdened with his own inevitable mortality. He could find no peace, and his divorce from any kind of religious panacea made his suffering worse. Yet Monro had the kind of sincerity and honesty which, if we are prepared to sympathetically engage with it, is a genuine revelation of one individual's inner life. And, strangely, he didn't appear to value any criticism of his poetry which wasn't just and honest. He wasn't looking for recognition in the conventional literary sense: he was looking for readers who valued and responded to what he was trying to do.

Eliot was absolutely convinced that Monro's poetry would 'remain' wherever and whenever discerning readers were prepared to encounter it. Monro's poetry was a significant contribution to that kind of poetry which is a permanent feature of individual human expression. As C.H. Sisson says in his *English Poetry 1900-1950*, Monro's later poetry 'came from a deeper interior' than his early verse and represents the 'authentic' expression of the man himself as he struggled for meaning.

I think it as well that (bearing in mind the studied judgement of T.S. Eliot) we consider the circumstances in which Harold Monro tried to write the poems that he did. He had money, he had influence, he had numerous literary friends and acquaintances, and he never found it difficult to get his own work published. But much – if not most – of his time was spent in supporting and encouraging other poets. He was intensely busy and was, one supposes, happy to be so. For someone so introspective and brooding, involvement in the sometimes hectic work of poetry publishing, where it was necessary not only to deal with very practical issues but to handle a range of what one might call 'poetic sensibilities and sensitivities', must have helped to take his mind off his own mental struggles. Although Monro was devoted to poetry and regarded himself as a serious poet, it cannot be assumed that he was necessarily comforted by the need to explore his inner self. There was a conflict between the need to express himself and the need to escape himself.

Yet there is no doubt that Monro had a devotion to the idea of 'poetry' which had remained with him from his late teens. He was, in youth, much influenced by a sort of Shelleyan idealism, and he spent much of his time, in his twenties, pursuing various fashionable extremes, both social and political. He was forced to leave school at the age of sixteen and, from that time, nourished himself extensively and intensively on poetry. And as he read, he became emotionally captivated by the idea of himself becoming a poet. From that time, his personal relationships were as much to do with feeding this passion for poetry as anything else. Such a passion brought him into contact with others whose main interests were socialism, or vegetarianism, or sexual liberation, or whatever, and one gets the impression that Monro became mixed up in all this because there was nowhere else to indulge his restless appetite for what seemed progressive or, at times, revolutionary. He just could not settle, and his flirtation with the Bar, with farming, with a life of physical and mental asceticism, were all attempts to find a home for what had become a passionate vocation. He was utterly devoted to poetry, spent much of his time reading, discussing, or writing it and, at the same time, seemed unable to reconcile such an idealism with the common practicalities of existence.

In a strange kind of way, though, that practicality was always there. But Monro was a creature of opposite and conflicting tendencies. F.S. Flint, who was one of the founders of Imagism and a pronounced influence on the poetic manner of the day, said that he was 'hardworking and lazy; he was generous and mean; he was a lover of freedom and a tyrant; unconventional and conventional; a bohemian and a bourgeois.' Flint was himself not unlike Monro, torn between poetic idealism and the pressures of the everyday world. But, unlike Flint, Monro belonged to no school. He was interested in all manifestations of what he might have called the poetic spirit, and managed to keep the peace between the various factions he was confronted by, both as a fellow poet and a publisher. Even this very unusual combination of diplomacy and sensitive tact may well have damaged his own reasonable claims for attention. At the Poetry Bookshop, he was used to encouraging young poets of every stylistic persuasion, and made a point of not getting too involved in literary prejudices and factional quarrels. He certainly had his own personal likes and dislikes, but he never forced them on anyone. He was prepared to say what he thought, when asked, but kept his peace when he felt it was necessary.

Harold Monro lived, day by day, in an atmosphere of literary ferment, and in the stormy seas on which he sailed he kept a firm and steady hand on the tiller. But, inside this rather solemn and seemingly balanced individual, battles were raging which became public only when the poems he wrote became available to his fellow poets and, later, to the poetry reading public. There were those, like Eliot and Flint, who knew what these poems cost him, and it is surely necessary for his poems to be once more fully exposed to a world whose constantly changing literary fashions and merciless concentration on commercial interests, too easily discards those who made a significant contribution to the poetic tradition. Harold Monro was one of those, and further examination of his singular contribution to English poetry will, hopefully, make this clearer.

But first we need to study in more detail his own personal history and the kind of world he found himself struggling to understand.

2
RESTLESSNESS

Harold Monro was born near Brussels in 1879. His father was a civil engineer who died when Monro was only ten years old. The Monro family were distinguished in more ways than one: a distant ancestor had been principal of Edinburgh University and there were several eminent physicians among his forebears. There was a tradition, too, of associating with artists. In the eighteenth century, Thomas Monro was a patron of painters like Turner, as well as being something of an artist as well. Harold's grandfather, the last in a long line of physicians, had a practice in Wimpole Street and Harold's own son, Nigel, became a doctor and carried on the family tradition. The family was definitely what we might call upper middle class and there was always a sense of social responsibility in whatever they put their minds to. When, after being sent to a preparatory school, Harold went on to become a pupil at Radley, a public school founded on High Church principles, it was hoped he would bring credit to an already distinguished family.

However, Harold's years at Radley appear to have been singularly insignificant and, at the age of sixteen, and much to the disappointment of his family, he had to leave the school quite suddenly having been found in possession of a bottle or two of wine. Mother, especially, was not impressed. And his uncle, who had married the daughter of a baronet, and resided in style at Somerby Hall, in Rutland, even less so. He himself had been a senior prefect at the school, a winner of the history prize, and a more than competent oarsman, as well as being a boxer at Oxford.

For the next two years Monro lived in a sort of dreamy world, gradually and then fervently influenced by his reading of poetry. He was a solitary adolescent and reading the poets became something of an obsession. He also began to write poems himself, stirred by his reading of Byron and Keats. These poems were more than short lyrics: he wrote a long poem entitled *The Madonna*, in rhyming couplets, for instance. He was conscious of himself as a poet: someone who was beginning a lifelong dedication to that art. Everything he did revolved around poetry and, assisted by tutors, he became familiar with poets like Milton and Tennyson, having already acquired a reading knowledge of Virgil. For someone so young, this kind of utterly focused interest was most certainly unusual, and the fact that he was writing poems daily is evidence that he had found his vocation.

When he went up to Cambridge to study medieval and modern languages he continued to write poems. But he kept this secret until his third year, when he formed a group with three other students to discuss work in progress. One of the students, Maurice Browne, became a very close friend and he and Monro remained in close contact for many years, sharing the same kind of idealism.

There was another side to Monro, though, and his addiction to horse racing, for instance, is a typical example of the apparent incompatibility of interests which he became famous for in later life. He was always a strange kind of split personality, and he attempted to reconcile the conflict between the two sides of his character in his poems. Yet he was never at peace, and his poems showed it.

Monro was a dedicated walker, and it was on long and sometimes arduous treks that his poems slowly gestated. He often discussed poetry and its relation to grand ideas with like-minded walking friends, especially Maurice Browne. On one special occasion (a walking tour in the Harz mountains) Browne brought along his younger sister, Dorothy. Harold, influenced by the circumstances and his own state of mind, fell in love, and it became almost inevitable that, in due course, they would get married.

After yet another unimpressive achievement, a Third in his Final examinations, Harold decided to impress his family by reading for the Bar, but he only passed a couple of Bar examinations before giving up the Law and becoming a land agent and small farmer in Ireland. Once there, he waited for Dorothy to join him and become his wife. However, she was a formidable hockey player, playing for England, and the thought of giving it all up to live on a remote farm in Ireland had little appeal for her. But this she did, with Harold determined to develop her mind and open it up to Beauty and Truth. Harold's only son, Nigel, was born there and the realities of their existence gradually began to frustrate all notions of pastoral idealism. Although Harold continued to write his poems, ride with the local Hunt and, generally, cultivate a pretence to the rural life, at heart he must have known this would never work. As he wrote in a letter to Maurice Browne, 'One wants a town sometimes, with theatres and particularly pictures and sculpture, and then there is this eternal rain.'

So, almost inevitably, the flirtation with country life came to an end. First his wife and son and then he himself returned to England, finally settling in a cottage in Haslemere. It was 1906 and Harold, with his own study and surrounded by his beloved books, was ready to seriously embark on a literary career.

Early that year, his brother-in-law and closest friend came up with the idea of the Samurai Press, the name itself indicative of the warrior ideals which fired the two young men. Harold was fully supportive, providing money and advice. The Samurai code included not only the publication of slim volumes of poetry but also a rather extreme form of asceticism which must, fundamentally, have felt somewhat foreign to the more rounded tastes of Monro: vegetarianism, early rising, teetotalism and non-smoking hardly describe the regular habits of the Monro of later years. But it was typical of him to become involved with such idealistic nonsense and, in any case, he felt that becoming part of it was the only way to get the kind of poetry he favoured into print. This proved false, almost immediately, and Harold soon began to see the folly of the publishing side of the code: it was easy enough to get poetry into print, but quite another matter to get it noticed. Browne, however, was not to be deterred. In 1907, the Press was installed in Ranworth Hall, near Norwich and, from there, issued an impossibly idealistic and impractical prospectus to which, probably against his truer nature, Monro contributed.

Proposals for a Voluntary Nobility somehow doesn't ring true to the Monro we discover through his poems. Anyway, after only four months, Browne had escaped overseas and left the whole show in charge of Arthur Sabin, a largely self-educated Sheffield steel worker who went on to establish himself as someone of contemporary importance as a poet, publisher, and museum official. He moved the outfit to Cranleigh in Surrey, near to where Monro lived. But even Sabin's competence and practicality only enabled the Press to survive for another two years or so.

By this time, Monro had become a Wellsian. He published a pamphlet entitled *The Evolution of the Soul* which denied the conventional religious beliefs he had been brought up to honour and suggested that man could cultivate his individual spirit outside traditional religious beliefs, regarding Jesus Christ as a spiritual teacher whose teachings had been perverted by the Church. He fortified this belief by publishing a long poem, *Judas*, with the intention to 'see as Judas saw, to understand as he understood, and to disclose his kinship with the money-victims of this and every age.' This long, and technically impressive poem, appears in his *Collected Poems*.

Meanwhile, Monro had come into contact with a movement which sought to embody the ideals represented by people like Ruskin and Morris: weavers, embroiderers, wood carvers, and so on. This movement fitted exactly Monro's idealistic, quasi-religious, beliefs about poetry. Art must be used for the improvement of mankind, and poetry would bring meaning and purpose to lives spoiled by more ephemeral and mercenary preoccupations. The whole ambience of Monro's Poetry

Bookshop, right down to the kind of furnishings he used, was a practical vindication of these ideals.

But his marriage had broken up and he had, like his friend Browne, escaped to the Continent. For the two years he was there, his ideals gestated in a fertile and active mind until, in 1909, he published, apart from a book of poetry, *Chronicle of a Pilgrimage: Paris to Milan on Foot*. He was thereby associating himself with the likes of Wordsworth, Coleridge and, especially, Shelley, emotionally and imaginatively stimulated by the grandeur of mountainous scenery. The nature of this impassioned description of his state of mind at the time reveals the way in which part of him was incurably romantic, with the consequent danger of a lapse into sentimentality. This is the tightrope which all his poetry insecurely navigates. He is only saved by his concentration on the real, even mundane, nature of the world he actually lived in. The tension between the two is what gives his poems life and importance.

His book of poems, *Before Dawn*, was printed by Arthur Sabin, and published in 1911. He was upset by the response to his attempt to reflect what he saw as real life, especially by Edward Thomas's suggestion that he might have done better to write in prose. Yet he claimed that the poems were 'felt' as poetry not as prose, and this feeling is particularly relevant to the true nature of Monro's work. He was after something which introduced problems which only he could resolve. And, at thirty-two, he felt the pressure of his years. When the famous historical novelist Maurice Hewlett experienced first-hand Monro's frustrations about the state of poetry and replied 'If you feel like that, for God's sake go back to England and do something', Monro was stung enough to be goaded into action. After two years travelling throughout Germany, Austria, and particularly Italy, and continuous intense discussion with well-known expatriate artists, novelists, and poets in various locations, Monro was ready to return to England and put his ideals into practice.

3

THEORY AND PRACTICE

Four months later, he was invited by the Poetry Society to edit the first number of *Poetry Review*. From this time, Monro began to move to the centre of the poetry world, a position he would control without embroiling himself in the embattled coteries which surrounded him. His own view of poetry remained resolutely idealistic: poetry wasn't about poets but about an activity which should be shared as widely as possible. In his way, he believed that everyone was able to write poems and poetry readers should have access to what they wrote wherever it was available. These ideas were behind both the founding of *Poetry Review* and the creation of the Poetry Bookshop. Yet, paradoxically, he soon became frustrated by the abundance which, in later years, he himself did so much to create.

The Poetry Society was founded in 1909, and devoted to the promotion of poetry by supporting poets, encouraging them, and arranging recitation courses. The Society had a very traditional view of poetry and it rapidly became a rather introverted assembly of mainly establishment people who specialised in self-cultivation and who had an exaggerated idea of their own importance. In that sense, it was very obviously patronising towards those it saw as lesser mortals. Instead of the people Monro was interested in, it gathered around it poets who had made names for themselves and who were bent on furthering their own interests. It was, in every sense, self-serving. At the same time, the Society encouraged the kind of poetry which failed to satisfy Monro's taste. He was looking for poems which challenged the prevailing fashion.

It was inevitable, therefore, that when Monro was offered the editorship of the recently founded *Poetry Review* he would refuse it. However, he was keen to get into publishing and, when the Society persisted in trying to capture him, Monro saw the opportunity of securing the editorship under his own terms. He needed enough independence to create a movement towards a more outward looking, more adventurous view of poetry, enlisting the support of liberal minds and, especially, younger poets. He rightly sensed that change was in the air, and he determined to take advantage of it.

When Monro finally accepted the editorship of the *Poetry Review* he had, in the background, a cohort of people who supported what he would try to achieve: people like Arthur Sabin and F.S. Flint. And Monro himself was a very efficient organiser who was capable of co-ordinating his gathering forces. He knew they were there. It was simply a matter of engineering the right kind of relationship with the Poetry Society: a relationship which suited him rather than them.

When the first number appeared, in 1912, it contained an article by him which expressed his own view of what needed to happen if his personal ambitions for poetry were to be successful. Poetry was 'the natural voice of the spirit' but 'today it is remote from life'. Poetry 'must be fundamental, vital, innate or nothing at all'. But beyond these sensible views, Monro, as was his wont, took flight into regions where few were able to follow him: 'words will sweep in flight across the world with the dignity and glorious symmetry of great flocks of birds' and so on.

In his preface to that issue, however, Monro revealed the coherent and practical character who, ultimately, triumphed over the Shelleyan idealist. It was time for the development of critical standards, and poetry should have the same status as the other arts. He wanted to 'create an atmosphere' where it was possible to form a base 'from which poetry at last emerges'. It was here, in this preface, that Monro established the importance of penetrating reviews and the beginnings of a culture of emerging critical values. Lots of poetry was being published but it had no direction. In a real sense, the quantity of new verse was swamping the poetry of quality which only discerning readers could identify. There seemed no point in indiscriminately adding to its volume. 'You cannot expect the public to turn over piles of rubbish to find something for itself,' Monro wrote to Harriet Monroe, the editor of the new American *Poetry (Chicago)*. She herself favoured publishing poems rather than reviews and critical essays.

There seems to be something of a contradiction here between Monro's seemingly open invitation to poets to write and readers to read, and this new emphasis on critical standards and discrimination. It continues throughout his whole career, where he attempts to be open and democratic and, at the same time, selective and restrictive. He had his own idea of what was a good poem yet was only too ready to publish poems which he, in all honesty, had little time for. Now, however, at this early stage of editing and publishing, he exhibited an underlying conservatism.

It is possible that the character of Monro's own poems were as much an example of uncertainty and confused personal identity as his critical pronouncements were. Even as a publisher, he seems to be unsure of exactly where he is going, and this uncertainty is possibly reflected in his openness to the views of what we can now see as 'modernist' practitioners, without actually taking sides. He lets things happen, in fact, under the disguise of determining what actually does happen. Perhaps this is what saved him as a poet, in the end: this undercurrent of 'negative capability'.

But he was driven by emotional idealism as well, and this is what gave him the stamina to do what he did. He steered an independent course, seemingly impervious to the pressures from people like Ezra Pound and the instigators of Imagism, as well as the extraordinary individualism of T.S. Eliot who, unlike Monro, knew exactly what he wanted to do and how to do it. In the end, Monro affected that he knew what they were about all along, although one suspects that he was learning and adapting rather than in spirited harmony. Behind his more revolutionary statements lurked the spirit of caution. But Pound, Hulme, Flint and, in the background Eliot, saw Monro as a convenient vehicle for promoting their own plans for conquering the publishing landscape and they found their place in the pages of *Poetry Review*. In a sense, they pirated the space Monro had established. But while Pound was able to define his 'Credo' there, and Flint his survey of modern French poetry, Rupert Brooke, a quite different poet, was made much of by receiving a monetary prize for the *Old Vicarage, Granchester*, a poem which later became much anthologised. Monro's panel of judges included Henry Newbolt, Ernest Rhys, Edward Thomas, Victor Plarr, Edward Marsh, and T.E. Hulme. Who but Monro could have brought such a motley crew together? And who but Monro could have somehow moved such an obviously comfortable poem into the spotlight? No wonder Pound stamped and fumed.

The Poetry Society, however, was not comfortable with what Monro was doing. Toward the end of 1912, matters came to a head. Monro's plans for *Poetry Review* gave the impression that it was within his remit to do what he liked. He was reminded that the journal was the property of the Poetry Society. Realising that his own independence as an editor was under threat, Monro relinquished his editorship and steered his contributors towards his own version, which became *Poetry and Drama*. *Poetry Review*, thereafter, returned to its old camp and continued to be comforting and uncontroversial for the next five or so decades. By 1913, *Poetry and Drama* was for sale, the Poetry Bookshop had been opened, and the first volume of *Georgian Poetry* had been issued, with Monro as its publisher. Now, at last, he was securely in control. But what he achieved in future would depend to a very large extent on the woman he married in 1920.

4

ALIDA MONRO

Alida Klementaski was seventeen years younger than Harold. She was of Polish descent and extremely beautiful. A photograph of her shows a rather heavy face, with a strong jaw, deep eyes and, curiously, the kind of absorbed serious expression Monro himself often wore. There is an uncanny resemblance, too, in their facial characteristics, which might suggest to a casual observer that they were related. Certainly, in a very short time, they became very close.

Alida, like Monro, needed a dominant purpose in life. She was looking for a project which she could devote herself to. Initially, she had intended to become a doctor, with the intention of saving fallen women from prostitution. But her need (again, like Monro's) to engage with the public, tempted her to try the stage. In the end, her gift for recitation, and her love of poetry, brought her into contact with Harold. She became a regular reader at the Poetry Bookshop and, eventually, Harold's secretary, where she revealed a talent for administration and business accounting. And when Harold was involved in his military duties during the First World War, Alida ran both the bookshop and the publishing side of Harold's career.

It was obvious that Harold was becoming increasingly dependent on Alida's support and it became inevitable that they would eventually marry. Harold himself does not appear to have been sexually drawn to Alida, but she somehow satisfied his intellectual needs. They were totally compatible as a partnership and, although neither subscribed to a conventional view of marriage, they both seemed to have felt that the strength of their relationship required some kind of official sanction. Alida kept her maiden name, and Harold allowed himself the freedom to live a kind of bachelor existence. But the times when they were together were of crucial importance to Harold.

Alida not only shared Harold's devotion to poetry; she also valued his work. It was she who always claimed that Harold's poetry was more important to him than anything else in his life. When she read his poems aloud at the Poetry Bookshop readings and elsewhere, it was obvious that she was able to communicate their emotional resonance.

It is natural for readers to wonder to what extent his more personal poems were specifically addressed to her. She herself always claimed that they were. For example, 'Hearthstone', a poem addressed to an absent 'Friend' was, she said, a genuine celebration of their life together and its crucial importance to Harold's happiness. His reference to the friend's 'hard thought', to the friend's 'great dog', to the dropped book of an avid reader who cannot send her 'brain to bed' and who is 'searching' – all these suggest what we know of Alida but, somehow, we are not totally convinced that the 'friend' is her.

But there is no doubt that without Alida Harold Monro would have lost an essential advocate. It was she who did everything to promote his poems both before and after his death. There is no evidence that her taste in poetry differed much from his. Her revision of *Twentieth Century Poetry*, after his death, was minor, and she had played a major part in the original selection, in addition to choosing the selection from Harold's poems. She chose 'Children of Love', 'The Quiet Mind', 'The Nightingale Near The House', 'Elm Angel', 'Midnight Lamentation', and an extract from 'Trees'. Her selection is interesting because she chose 'Midnight Lamentation' as one of the poems. This poem is possibly the most intimate of Harold's poems, and Alida must have found the last stanza of particular significance:

> I cannot find a way
> Through love and through;
> I cannot reach beyond
> Body, to you.
> When you or I must go
> Down evermore,
> There'll be no more to say
> – But a locked door.

This very fine poem explores Harold's need for closeness and intimacy, as well as his horror of loss and death. What seems to have intensely troubled him was the impossibility of ever truly knowing another human being. Some of the other love poems have the same intensity as this one: 'Where She Lives', for instance. They are tense and disturbed, and tend to emphasize the distance between the lovers, and the sense of being alone in spite of being together. 'Great Distance' is a poem which describes, very directly and effectively, what it feels like to be separated from a lover and, at the same time, the need to believe in love's reality. What strikes the reader most, in these and other love poems ('Silence Between', 'New Day', 'Unto Her', 'The One Faithful', 'Love in the Autumn Forest', 'In the Night', 'Unanswered Question', and 'The Terrible Door', to give a few examples) is Monro's sense of the impossibility of a permanent and stable condition of happiness between two lovers. It was not so much the death of love itself, but the impossibility of its permanence which so troubled him. He could never take any intimate relationship for granted – never relax and enjoy it – because he was always conscious of time and mortality. Desperate as he was to find security and permanence, it always evaded him.

I don't think it really matters whether or not these love poems are addressed to Alida. Even if they (or some of them) are addressed to someone else, they matter because they are intensely felt. They all reflect Monro's essential problem: the evanescence of everything, the transitory and ephemeral nature of experience (in spite of the solidity of objects, an idea he often plays with) and the way in which even the presence of the beloved cannot ultimately solve the existential dilemma which haunts him. Is it, after all, a dream? Alida was such a firm and permanent figure in his life, always there when he needed her and very much part of the intimate and domesticated retreats they both cherished, away from that other noisy and demanding literary world they also shared. But was it all real? What did it all mean?

When Alida chose and edited the *Collected Poems*, it was she who decided that the poems should be printed with the later poems first, presumably because it was in these poems that she saw the truest expression of Monro's gift. Her own selection for *Twentieth Century Poetry* is, however, a confusing choice. One wonders, sometimes, if she failed to understand the depth of Harold's troubled emotions. For example, she insisted that 'Bitter Sanctuary' describes Harold's experiences in hospital, whereas its original title 'The Alcoholics' suggests otherwise. Again, she strongly refuted Richard Aldington's description of her husband's drunken behaviour (described in *Life for Life's Sake*) when, in fact, Aldington's narrative is undeniably authentic. It is as if she always needed to claim her ownership of Harold's mental existence and, perhaps, this is central to Harold's own neurotic disturbances, reflected most obviously in his excessive drinking.

We learn, from a BBC broadcast which Alida gave in 1955, of Harold's 'rigid belief that this life is all, and there is no future beyond the grave'. And she wrote to Sturge Moore, not long after Harold's death, that Harold feared absolute extinction. It is not uncommon for alcoholics to escape from this existential problem by losing themselves in alcoholic paralysis. Alida herself seems so much the stronger character of the two but, paradoxically, this strength may have somewhat blinded her to Harold's fundamental problems.

When she first met him, Alida must have been impressed with Harold's obviously influential position in the literary world of the early twentieth century. She was then 22 years old, and relished the chance to become involved in his work. In doing so, she found a satisfactory resolution of her own ambitions and became, fairly rapidly, essential to his literary and business activities. She was never reluctant to take over whatever responsibilities Harold gave her and, in due course, gave him the kind of stability and security he craved.

According to F.S. Flint, in his biographical introduction to the first *Collected Poems*, Alida managed to convince Harold that his 'phantasms and illusions' were unnecessary and 'from the beginning of his association with Alida Klemantaski a change appeared in his verses'. I don't see how one can verify this, and Alida's selection of 'Children of Love', for *Twentieth Century Poetry* would seem to contradict this assertion. Surely, if Alida had been really confident of Harold's true worth as a poet she would not have chosen such an early example of the kind of 'phantasm and illusion' that 'Children of Love' represents. It is a poem that does no justice to Harold Monro as a significant twentieth-century poet.

Of course, the history of Monro's own life would have been somewhat different if Alida had never become a part of it. She looked after him when he was ill, she ran his business when he was otherwise engaged, she kept his literary affairs alive. But did she really understand this man who appears to have become so emotionally dependent on her? The fact that she was jealous of his reputation and zealous of protecting it after his untimely death doesn't mean that she was his best critic. At the heart of her relationship with Harold lie questions we shall never be able to answer. His later poems reflect his intense emotional need for love and the desolation of a life separated from the security which intimacy provides. Monro's reserve about obviously identifying her with the person he was in love with suggests that, fundamentally, she did not satisfy his emotional needs. A lover is more than a 'Friend'.

Somehow, Monro seems a repressed character who needed alcohol to release him from his introversion and social inhibitions. He delighted in horse riding, riding motorbikes, and domestic pets – all, perhaps, a disguise which protected his own emotional vulnerability. One senses his satisfaction at the way Alida was able to laugh about things, to mingle easily with all sorts of people, to handle difficult social situations and, generally, to take charge of his affairs. When he was in any kind of trouble, it was always Alida who would sort things out. She was a nurse as well as a business partner. She managed to convince him that she understood what he was exploring in his better poems, and she read them so well that he had concrete evidence of this. However, Monro could never have written those later poems if he had been completely certain of her understanding.

Monro was a large man, with a commanding physical presence, although he made no effort to assert it. There is no reason to doubt that he must also have been a man with a healthy sexual appetite. Yet, in his poems, there is no evidence of this. His poems about sexually frustrated nuns, in 'To the Ladies of the Convent', and to sexually timid Christians, in 'The Curate's Christmas Eve', are written from a confident distance. We are allowed to make the assumption that Monro's own sexual appetites are conventionally normal. But something was always missing.

There is nothing in the poems which explores physical love in any depth. We have no idea whether Monro was keen to explore such a love, or even whether he himself had experience of such love. What we do know is that he needed understanding. His best poems explore his own isolation and his emotional needs. And it is his struggle to express the complexity of those needs which give some of his later poems their power.

Whether or not we believe that Harold's love poems were written to anyone other than Alida, there is no doubt whatsoever that she did give Monro the security and stability to explore his own confusions as far as he was able, and to promote his efforts to do so. But it is questionable whether she really understood the reasons for his alcoholism. She herself comes across as a forceful and balanced personality, and it was her normality which preserved Harold from self-destruction. And she did everything in her power to preserve his memory and to keep his poems in literary currency. For that, we have to be grateful.

5

THE POETRY BOOKSHOP

By the time Harold Monro started the Poetry Bookshop, he had already gained something of a reputation as a poet. His first substantial collection, *Before Dawn*, published by Constable in 1911, had been preceded by the publication of his long poem, *Judas*, under the Samurai imprint, and there had been an even earlier small pamphlet *Poems*, which had been published by Elkin and Matthews in 1906. His poems had appeared in various periodicals, including his own *Poetry Review*. His ownership of the Poetry Bookshop gave him the opportunity of not only publishing poets he approved of, but also collections of his own work. He was thus in a very strong position indeed to effect the kinds of change in the poetry scene which he believed necessary. He had also collected around him a powerful group of individuals who were directly concerned with promoting their own ideas of what this scene should look like. It was his ability to balance the energies that he was surrounded by to his own advantage which contributed to his success.

There was a picture of the Poetry Bookshop on the cover of Monro's *Poetry and Drama*, a sign that he was consolidating his own position. In an early issue, the National Anthem was attacked as 'one of the holiest institutions of Empire' and it was suggested that the Laureateship should be abolished, since it was incompatible with the sort of poetry that Monro approved of. In other words, Monro was concentrating on bringing down the kind of poetry establishment which frustrated all efforts at change and development. If the battle for poetry was to be opened up, then everything had to begin with a level playing field, and Monro aimed to provide it. In *Poetry and Drama*, he aimed for an enlightened middle course for poetry, avoiding the dead weight of the inherited poetry establishment and the fervent energies of the revolutionary wing. By doing so, he perhaps blurred the outlines somewhat, so that the picture represented by his own anthology *Twentieth Century Poetry* (1929) is a confusing mixture of the old and the new, of major and minor talents, of the traditional and the experimental. One would have expected this substantial and mature selection to be more exciting and fresh than it actually is.

The collections of *Georgian Poetry*, commissioned by Edward Marsh and published by the Poetry Bookshop, further confuse the sort of poetry that Monro wished to promote. Both Edward Marsh and Monro himself wanted to support the developing movement towards a new kind of poetry, but Edward Marsh had his own very definite views of what poetry should look like, and the huge success of the first issue put the ball securely in his court. When Marsh brought together the people he felt could most contribute to the idea of a new kind of poetry, he included

Rupert Brooke, John Drinkwater, W.W. Gibson, and Arundel del Re, as well as Monro himself. Neither Drinkwater nor Gibson was published individually under the Poetry Bookshop imprint and there is little evidence that Monro was particularly interested in their poems. In fact, his comments on their poetry in his *Some Contemporary* Poets (1920) are more than a little disparaging. Brooke, of course, was a different matter.

But there was a driving philosophy behind the creation of *Georgian Poetry* and the poets who were involved in the project were aware of it. What, then, was this philosophy? It was, to quote John Press in his *A Map of Modern English Verse*, a reaction to 'the fag-end of Victorian rhetoric and the entrenched forces of literary conservatism led by such men as Newbolt, Noyes, Alfred Austin and William Watson.' The new young poets were even criticised for 'their determination at all costs to be original.' But they were also encouraged by Robert Bridges, a considerably older poet and, oddly it seems to us today, by some of the poets who were sympathetic towards Imagism, like D.H. Lawrence, who actually appeared in the *Georgian Poetry* series.

The lines, in fact, are somewhat blurred. We might see Edward Marsh's poets as being 'poets (who) were content to employ the conventions of diction and the forms of verse favoured by almost all English poets from Wordsworth to Hardy' and who 'looked for guidance to Milton, the major Romantics, and the Victorians', to quote from *A Map of Modern English Verse*. But that is only partly true of the poets themselves, although it may better describe Marsh's own taste. And if they also 'felt an intuitive sympathy with the specifically English elements of English poetry rather than its European aspects' and, most pertinent of all, 'remained ignorant, indifferent or hostile to the revolution in sensibility and technique inaugurated by Pound and Eliot' that was not wholly the case with Monro who, after all, was not responsible for the contents of the series.

Monro himself was prepared to survey the whole field of poetry to discover which poets genuinely appealed to him. Indeed, he later did this in order to produce his *Twentieth Century Poetry*. For that anthology, he read through 'all the books published' in the twentieth century up to then (1929), 'and most of those published towards' the end of the century before. All in all, 'about 600 volumes' were 'read or re-read, to refresh the memory'. The introduction to the collection ended with the words: 'I have thought of the book in terms of a Building. You are left to judge the main proportions. Above all, may it delight you'. For most readers such a comprehensive collection exhausts rather than stimulates. Somehow, it is so typically Monro.

Certainly, such an exhortation did little to clarify the way poetry might develop in the near future, and it is fair, I think, to conclude that Monro himself had no clear views about this. It was enough for him to pin his standard to the mast of poetry itself, giving it a kind of meaningless religious aura. In the process, he may well have stained his own reputation as a poet to be preserved and read, his potential readership becoming increasingly convinced that he belonged essentially to *Georgian Poetry* and the philosophy which pervaded it, which he most certainly did not.

In reviewing *Georgian Poetry (1915-1917)* T.S. Eliot, writing under a pseudonym, wrote in *The Egoist*, 'What nearly all the writers have in common is the quality of pleasantness. There are two kinds of pleasantness: (1) the insidiously didactic or

Wordsworthian (a rainbow and a cuckoo's song): (2) the decorative, playful or solemn, minor-Keatsian, too happy, happy brook ... '. Monro, as a kind of collaborator with Marsh, and a regular contributor to the series, must obviously come under scrutiny, and it might help if we examine his attitude to Eliot himself and also to Edward Thomas.

To begin with Thomas. To a sensitive, perceptive intelligence, Thomas was a poet who wrote with a fine distinction between the crude and evanescent and the pure and permanent, which is why he is still read today. There is absolutely nothing in his style which is dramatically modernist, nothing which betrays a desire to be fashionable and current. He wrote his very fine poems because he had to, because he needed to explore his own emotions, and in doing so he used language with exquisite subtlety, feeling and intellect running closely together. Of all poets, this should have been the poet Monro instinctively aligned himself with. But he missed the call. Having secured him as a reviewer and critic, Monro failed to recognise his distinction as a poet. When Thomas sent Monro a few poems in 1914, Monro kept them for four days and then said that he hadn't had time to read them. And the following year, when Thomas sent him quite a bundle, hoping that he might make a book of them, he rejected them outright. One can only imagine the effect on Thomas. Paradoxically, after Thomas's death, Monro wrote to his widow, Helen, finally offering to publish them. Helen's reply clearly expresses Thomas's hurt at those two refusals, as well as her pleasure that another publisher had already accepted them. In a way typically, Monro had waited too long for others' approval before making his decision as, indeed, he did with Eliot.

When the American poet, Conrad Aiken, offered Monro Eliot's *The Love Song of J. Alfred Prufrock*, Monro said that the poem was 'absolutely insane, or words to that effect'. And when Aiken showed him 'La Figlia Che Piange', Monro was intensely irritated, and gave it back to him, saying he couldn't be bothered with it. Yet, once Eliot's reputation as a significant modernist had been established, Monro gladly went along with it. He published six of Eliot's poems in his anthology *Twentieth Century Poetry*.

Pound, who could recognise a poem when he saw one, was often frustrated by Monro's slowness to respond to poems which, in Pound's view, were so obviously of real worth. 'Even Monro's Devonshire Street occiput has been pierced' he said, when Monro had at last modified his views about Eliot's poetry.

For some years, beginning in 1919 and continuing until 1925, Monro published a series of chapbooks (*The Monthly Chapbook* – later to appear less frequently) but, in spite of a good first issue, the series soon appeared to be going nowhere. Monro seemed to be ready to publish almost everybody and even approached J.C. Squire, the very epitome of the Georgian circle, for material. 'Bring your bloody CB to Paris,' wrote Pound, 'and try to collect a real team of contributors and perhaps something might be done about it'. 'Only HELL,' continued Pound, 'you never had a programme – you've always dragged in Aberbubble and Siphon, and Wobbleberry and wanted to exploit the necropolis.'

Sadly, Pound was once again on the ball. In spite of his seemingly calm presence at the Poetry Bookshop readings, his very democratic and non-partisan demeanour, and his generosity to younger talents than himself, Monro had no idea really where he was actually heading. He was surrounded by people who had much firmer ideas than he had, but who hadn't his practical ability to handle people and organise things. It was open house at the Poetry Bookshop. You could come and go as you liked. You could rely on Harold Monro's generosity when you really needed it. You could pick and choose your poets. But if you wanted signs of direction and purpose in all this, you were disappointed. It was all, in the end, just too comfortable.

However, Monro's failure to break new ground as a publisher and – to use today's term – his skill as a 'poetry facilitator', served his clientele well and satisfied a generation of poetasters. Yet, in the end, his success was responsible for his downfall. As Georgianism went out of fashion, so did Harold Monro. And with it went a poet who was so much more than his public image, and so much more than the poetry world he established and nurtured.

Behind all this desire to further the cause of poetry and to help poets to get into print, and behind his public image as a poetry benefactor, there was a true poet desperate to resolve his own emotional and intellectual struggles and to express, as honestly as he was able, the acute mental suffering which troubled him all his life. He was to make a long journey to develop a personal poetic manner which fitted what he was after, and his *Collected Poems* is a record of that journey. Only as he neared the end of it, does it become clear to discerning readers that here is a poet who is as important as Eliot said all those years ago: here is a poet who 'is more clearly the real right thing than any of the poetry of a somewhat older generation of mine except Mr Yeats's.' And he adds: 'In the end it will remain.'

No poet can be condemned simply because he happens to be

born at a particular time in history and is subject to the poetic conventions of his time. Of course, in hindsight, it's easy to see which poets somehow managed to avoid becoming the victims of contemporary poetic conventions. A poet like Blake owes absolutely nothing to the convention of composing verse in rhyming couplets, and Hopkins absolutely avoided becoming a typical Victorian poet. Most poets, however, find it necessary, for various reasons, to follow the fashions of the time. Others find it more convenient to join rebellious cliques. But Monro was open and generous enough to avoid being demonstratively partisan and, because he happened to be writing at a time when poetic fashions were particularly volatile, his diplomacy and tact damaged his subsequent reputation as a poet. But, throughout his writing life and right up to his death, he was striving to express his own individuality in his own particular way. This selection is based on the conviction that the time has now come to reassess the poetry of Harold Monro and bring it once more into focus.

6

THE POEMS

I suppose the burning question is: why is it that Harold Monro's poems are almost totally forgotten these days? And this question is linked to a further question: why are so many poets who happened to be writing in the earlier part of the twentieth century disregarded as serious poets? Both questions, it seems to me, are related to the position of T.S. Eliot as a central figure in the development of what we might call, for want of a better term, 'modernism'.

Eliot, of course, was not only a poet but a publisher. It is, therefore, important to remember that he not only thought Monro's poems of some worth but also published them himself. Eliot was a discerning editor and a publisher of scrupulous taste, and he published Monro and prefaced his *Collected Poems* because he regarded Monro as being different from his contemporaries in certain essential respects. What were these?

To summarise Eliot's criticism of certain kinds of poetry in a few words is virtually impossible, and it would entail looking in some detail at the many talks, lectures, essays and books that embody those ideas. However, it does no damage to Eliot's reputation to accept that the thing that made him most uncomfortable about the poems of his contemporaries in the early twentieth century was that they were too easy: they appeared to have been written without cost, as it were. As a poet who needed to find his own way of saying things, his search for models led him outside those currently available. Instead, he rediscovered the poets of the seventeenth century, where both intellect and emotion struggled for some kind of reconciliation. Poets like Donne, for instance.

A glance at some of the poets and poems included in the *Georgian Poetry* series, edited by Edward Marsh and published by Monro, gives one a pretty clear idea of what Eliot was rebelling against: poems like W.H. Davies's 'Sweet Stay-At-Home', with lines like:

> Sweet Stay-At-Home, sweet Love-one-place.
> Sweet, simple maid, bless thy dear face ...

Or James Stephens's:

> 'Play to the tender stops, though cheerily:
>   Gently, my soul, my song: let no one hear:
> Sing to thyself alone: thine ecstasy ... '

and so on, and so on.

Of course, not all the poems in *Georgian Poetry* were like this. Marsh also chose poets like D.H. Lawrence, Robert Graves, Siegfried Sassoon and Walter de la Mare: poets who, although not entirely free from the relaxed ease of their seemingly complacent contemporaries, attempted a subtlety and complexity which their contemporaries shunned. And, of course, Monro himself was a regular contributor to the *Georgian Poetry* series, exhibiting both the best and the worst of his work: poems like 'Overheard On A Saltmarsh' ('Nymph, nymph, what are your beads?/Green glass, goblin. Why do you stare at them?') as well as the infinitely superior 'Solitude' ('A distant engine whistles, or the floor/Creaks, or the wandering night-wind bangs a door.')

But Monro was as unsure about his own better poems as he was about the poems of others. In his anthology *Twentieth Century Poetry* (1929), for which he read or re-read 600 volumes, he selected poets like T.S. Eliot, Ezra Pound, Wilfred Owen, Isaac Rosenberg, and Edward Thomas alongside poets like Lascelles Abercrombie, Rupert Brooke, Eden Phillpotts, and Henry Newbolt. No wonder later readers became confused. So what was Monro trying to do in his poems? And what were his problems?

From the age of sixteen onwards, Monro read a lot of poetry. He read poems daily, and he wrote poems every day, too. The result was that he became quite fluent in style. His early long poem, *Judas*, exemplifies this. Here is a poem of some seven hundred or so lines which clearly demonstrates Monro's versatility and technical skill. It was written round about 1906, when Monro was twenty-seven. The whole poem flows easily from the pen of a seriously accomplished poet:

> So we passed northward, dreaming a land
> All summer-scented, reaching in the end
> The master's country, lovely Galilee.
> We prophesied the kingdom. When he preached
> We stood about him listening, waiting.

The half-rhyme, the easy movement from line to line, the subtle variation in the stressing, the skilfully placed short statements within the line, all give the movement of the verse pace and variation. It's extraordinary how different this is from Monro's later stylistic experiments, where he struggles, with varying degrees of success, to get close to what he feels. His surviving hand-written manuscripts are evidence of this struggle, dense as they are with crossings-out, corrections, and verbal substitutions.

Monro could, and did, from time to time, produce poems which were models of accomplished technique (like, for instance, 'Suburb' and the superbly fluent 'Impressions') as well as seemingly clumsy poems (like 'The Quiet Mind'). The real question is, why was Monro prepared to move away from accomplished and fluent traditional forms towards these more awkward expressions of his feelings? It's obvious, from the kinds of poems he was happy to publish, that he liked and admired poems which were almost banal in their conventionality, and that he, at least initially, had problems with poems which were experimental.

Personally, I think his indecisions were an essential part of the man himself and give his better poems their valuable authenticity. Monro was not an Auden, fluent and happy in a wide variety of modes and styles. He was, if anything, more of a Spender: a worrier over who and what he was and where, if at all, he fitted into the scheme of things. He had the same kind of sensitivity, too: a combination of intellectual sophistication and awkward naivety.

There is something in some poets (Herbert Read is a good

example, and Isaac Rosenberg might be another) which most poetry readers are reluctant to tolerate. Most readers of poetry enjoy poems which are easy to read and relaxing, if you like, rather than disturbing. This was, in fact, why *Georgian Poetry* did so well, at least initially. It was only when a newer generation of experimentalists and, later, politically engaged poets, began to dominate that poetry lost its relatively large readership. There was an absolute division between readers of, say, *The Poetry Review*, and readers of magazines like Eliot's *Criterion*. The *Criterion* died, but *Poetry Review* kept both its readership and its circulation. There has always been a readership and, these days, an audience for easier poetry.

Strangely, Monro wasn't interested in poets who cultivated their personalities. He detested those who seemed more interested in poets than in poems. You would have thought that someone who planted himself in the centre of the current 'poetry world', and who made much of poets being given a platform to read their own work, would have made more of the different poetic 'characters' he was surrounded by. But he didn't. He wasn't at all interested in W.H. Davies as a 'tramp poet' or whatever; he was interested only in his poems. He was always prepared to help poets out, and even give them space to live in, but his main preoccupation was the cause of poetry itself.

Monro was odd. People knew he was odd. And behind his somewhat dark and restrained manner was a man who, almost secretly, explored himself. He didn't really know who he was:

> Does not my ghost appear?
> My eyes feel over intervening space,
> And I am leaning forward at the strain

> Till, now, my fingers nearly touch your face.
> Lean out to me: I'm calling with my brain.

This stanza, from 'Silence Between' is a good example of the mental country the emotionally isolated Monro inhabited. He was an atheist, a convinced evolutionist, and a fervent devotee of the kind of future imagined by people like H.G. Wells. He believed that science held the key to the door which he would have liked to open, but couldn't. In its place was another door:

> Happy release! Good-bye for ever!
> Here at the corner we say good-bye.
> But if you want me, if you need me,
> Who waits, at the terrible door, but I?

The poem, 'The Terrible Door', like 'Silence Between', is a poem which explores the despair of an individual who is desperate for understanding and intimacy. Monro knew that a 'modern' belief in scientific progress would never solve his personal insecurity. Even his devotion to 'poetry' could never solve it. The only solution was to explore, in his own poems, what actually haunted him. And it is the poems which most faithfully do that which establish Monro's significance for us today.

Even in the much anthologised 'Milk for the Cat' Monro himself is felt within the lines. The description of the cat's lust for milk is extraordinarily intense:

> But the cat is grown small and thin with desire,
> Transformed to a creeping lust for milk.

The 'long dim ecstasy' which 'holds' the cat's life is Monro's own transposed dream of losing himself in that 'world' of 'infinite shapeless white'. Never, throughout the whole poem, does Monro mention himself in relation to the cat. He gives himself up utterly to the cat's world as he imagines it. It's a world uncontaminated by thought. It's the kind of world D.H. Lawrence created when he wrote about animals.

Again, in his poem 'Goldfish', Monro imagines a world which 'cannot pierce the barrier of Mind':

> Their eyes stare out from far away behind,
> And cannot pierce the barrier of Mind.
> In the same house are they and we;
> Yet well might be
> Divided by a whole Eternity!

In this extraordinary poem, Monro describes how 'you can feel':

> Their movements growing larger in the gloom,
> And merging with the room, and you are brought
> Back where they live, the other side of thought.

It is 'thought' which disturbs the possibility of innocence, of being 'the angels of that watery world.' For Monro, thought is a plague which contaminates the desire for peace and innocence.

There's that 'door', too. It appears explicitly in more than one poem. In 'London Interior' 'One dare not open this old door too wide;/It is so dark inside'; in 'Solitude' 'the wandering night-wind bangs a door'; in 'Fate' there is 'the locked door, the door I cannot open'; in 'Crossing a Bridge' there is 'a cry beyond an iron unopened door'; in 'Rumour' 'many whisper close outside some door'; and, in 'Midnight Lamentation', in the end, 'There'll be no more to say/ – But a locked door'. It's always the door that separates us, as in 'Great Distance' it separated Monro from the lover who stands 'just outside/My body's door'. And, in 'Bitter Sanctuary' the sick are left '(to what torture) waiting at the door' and, even when 'the door opens' there is still the same isolation expressed in 'Silence Between', where the lover cries 'Lean out to me: I'm calling with my brain'.

In this word 'brain' Monro seems to encapsulate the prison he appears to have made for himself by intellectually capitulating to the prevailing scientific materialism which had become fashionable. It's a strange word to use in poems, even for today's readers, and Monro uses it often. When he uses it, he describes his own isolation. In 'Officers' Mess' he speaks of his need to find 'a brain with which my brain may talk'. Later, in the same poem, he writes about the 'passages of Thought' where 'thought' is spelled with a capital letter. Monro is fond of capitalised abstractions: Love, Heaven, Peace, Death, and so on. This is a weakness and such usage somehow symbolises a kind of failure of poetic nerve. It was part of the literary custom of his day to slip into comfortable abstractions. The important thing about Monro, however, is the way he uses uncomfortable words like 'brain' to engage with the kind of reality he was trying to make sense of, instead of avoiding the issue. He is at his very best when he focuses on the exact and confronts the realities of his existence. This is what makes the well-regarded 'Bitter Sanctuary' so important. Throughout the poem, Monro concentrates on detail: 'the plush is nicotined', the woman 'licks her varnished thin magenta lips', 'heat has locked the heavy earth', and there is 'thin giggling from behind that shutter'. The same focus on details is what makes his poems about cats and dogs (although somewhat derided these days) good poems.

Nowhere is this detail more significant than in his descriptions of city life. Monro was a creature of the city. He would, by choice, have lived nowhere else, and his forays into the country always left him dissatisfied. When Monro combines exact urban description and his own mental unease he exemplifies one of the characteristics which, I'm sure, Eliot admired. Because, in fact, that was what Eliot himself often attempted to do. The poem 'London Interior' reminds one of the London Eliot describes in, for instance, 'Rhapsody on a Windy Night' or 'Morning at the Window'. But Monro never once imitates Eliot. His London is his own, as is the city home from which he experiences it: at a time when 'Autumn is in the air' and 'the hall smells of dust', 'the floor creaks' and 'a narrow squirt of sunlight enters high'. He can see 'the dingy garden with its wall and tree' and hear 'a woman call/Some child from play', and sense time 'ticking slow, glooming slow' and how:

> It is sad in London when the gloom
> Thickens, like wool,
> In the corners of the room ...

And the poem finally describes how 'the chairs creak' and 'The sunlight lays a streak upon the floor.'

Monro's descriptions of suburbia are very fine. 'Suburb' is particularly impressive and, once again, one is reminded of Eliot (shades of *The Waste Land*?):

> Here on warm nights the daughter brings
> Her vacillating clerk,

To talk of small exciting things
And touch his fingers through the dark.

The young man offers her 'Hopeless immense Hereafters' and, as 'the train is whistling past/He takes her in his arms at last.'

Probably the best of Monro is where he combines exact urban description with his own kind of mental unease, as in 'Evening':

Now the cool twilight, glowing,
Falls like dew
Upon the city's brow.
Now fretful day is slowing;
Slowly the river flows, but men are going
Swiftly, as though they knew
At last some hope beyond all silence.

But, for Monro, as he puts it in 'Great City':

When all the lamps were lighted in the town
I passed into the streetways, and I watched,
Wakeful, almost happy,
And half the night I wandered in the street.

Like Robert Frost, Monro was 'one acquainted with the night'.

I have tried to bring together poems which contain the true nature of the man himself, as far as we can know it. But a poet like Monro can never be securely captured. All his relatively short life he seems to have been gnawed by a restlessness which ate at his very being. Wherever he was, whether abroad, or having a weekend break in the country, or presiding over one of his poetry evenings at The Poetry Bookshop, he was never at peace. It was a peace which he could only imagine. As for the dead:

Some may be found, they say, deeply asleep
In ruined tombs.
Some in white beds, with faces round them. Some
Wander the world, and never find a home.

A SELECTION OF POEMS

A NOTE ON THE POEMS

There are two *Collected Poems* in existence, though both are long out of print. The first, published by Cobden-Sanderson in 1933, includes a valuable biographical sketch by F.S. Flint and a critical note by T.S. Eliot. The second *Collected Poems* was a reprint of the first, but excluded the pieces by Flint and Eliot. These were replaced by a Preface, written by Ruth Tomalin. The reprint was published by Duckworth in 1970. Both collections are, unfortunately, in reverse chronological order, which obscures the gradual development of Monro's individual gift. The reprint follows exactly the punctuation, orthography and layout of the 1933 *Collected Poems* which, unfortunately, is the only original to work from. I have been tempted to edit this but decided, in the end, to tolerate any obvious eccentricities. It seemed proper to do this, if only as a tribute to the individuality of Harold Monro. But my selection is in chronological order, as far as we know it. Hopefully, it reveals Monro's poetic development. Readers who want to explore Monro's poems further will have to rely on the two versions of the collected poems. A number of the poems are explored in Joy Grant's *Harold Monro and the Poetry Bookshop* (Routledge and Kegan Paul, 1967) from which I have taken much of my biographical information. This invaluable book is also out of print. The literary background to the poems can usefully be researched by reading the relevant parts of John Press's *A Map of English Verse* (Oxford, 1969). Apart from these sources, further information about Harold Monro can be found by trawling the internet but, unfortunately, such information is extremely limited.

My selection excludes poems which are obviously Georgian in approach and style, except for a few poems which are stubbornly attractive, however much they reflect the poetic fashion of the time. I have not given automatic space to anthology pieces.

THE POETS ARE WAITING

To what God
Shall we chant
Our songs of Battle?

The professional poets
Are measuring their thoughts
For felicitous sonnets;
They try them and fit them
Like honest tailors
Cunning materials
For fashion-plate suits.

The unprofessional
Little singers,
Most intellectual,
Merry with gossip,
Heavy with cunning,
Whose tedious brains are draped
In sultry palls of hair,
Reclining as usual
On armchairs and sofas,
Are grinning and gossiping,
Cake at their elbows –
They will not write us verses for the time;
Their storms are brewed in teacups and their wars
Are fought in sneers or little blots of ink.

To what God
Shall we chant
Our songs of Battle?

Hefty barbarians,
Roaring for war,
Are breaking upon us;
Clouds of their cavalry,
Waves of their infantry,
Mountains of guns.
Winged they are coming,
Plated and mailed,
Snorting their jargon.
Oh, to whom shall a song of battle be chanted?
Not to our lord of the hosts on his ancient throne,
Drowsing the ages out in Heaven alone.
The celestial choirs are mute, the angels have fled:
Word is gone forth abroad that our lord is dead.

To what God
Shall we chant
Our songs of battle?

MILK FOR THE CAT

When the tea is brought at five o'clock
And all the neat curtains are drawn with care,
The little black cat with bright green eyes
Is suddenly purring there.

At first she pretends, having nothing to do,
She has come in merely to blink by the grate,
But, though tea may be late or the milk may be sour,
She is never late.

And presently her agate eyes
Take a soft large milky haze,
And her independent casual glance
Becomes a stiff hard gaze.

Then she stamps her claws or lifts her ears
Or twists her tail and begins to stir,
Till suddenly all her lithe body becomes
One breathing trembling purr.

The children eat and wriggle and laugh;
The two old ladies stroke their silk:
But the cat is grown small and thin with desire,
Transformed to a creeping lust for milk.

The white saucer like some full moon descends
At last from the clouds of the table above;

She sighs and dreams and thrills and glows,
Transfigured with love.

She nestles over the shining rim,
Buries her chin in the creamy sea;
Her tail hangs loose; each drowsy paw
Is doubled under each bending knee.

A long dim ecstasy holds her life;
Her world is an infinite shapeless white,
Till her tongue has curled the last holy drop,
Then she sinks back into the night,

Draws and dips her body to heap
Her sleepy nerves in the great arm-chair,
Lies defeated and buried deep
Three or four hours unconscious there.

SUBURB

Dull and hard the low wind creaks
Among the rustling pampas plumes.
Drearily the year consumes
Its fifty-two insipid weeks.

Most of the grey-green meadow land
Was sold in parsimonious lots;
The dingy houses stand
Pressed by some stout contractor's hand
Tightly together in their plots.

Through builded banks the sullen river
Gropes, where its houses crouch and shiver.
Over the bridge the tyrant train
Shrieks, and emerges on the plain.

In all the better gardens you may pass,
(Product of many careful Saturdays),
Large red geraniums and tall pampas grass
Adorn the plots and mark the gravelled ways.

Sometimes in the background may be seen
A private summer-house in white or green.
Here on warm nights the daughter brings
Her vacillating clerk,
To talk of small exciting things
And touch his fingers through the dark.

He, in the uncomfortable breach
Between her trilling laughters,
Promises, in halting speech,
Hopeless immense Hereafters.

She trembles like the pampas plumes.
Her strained lips haggle. He assumes
The serious quest ...

Now as the train is whistling past
He takes her in his arms at last.

It's done. She blushes at his side
Across the lawn – a bride, a bride.

The stout contractor will design,
The lazy labourers will prepare,
Another villa on the line;
In the little garden-square
Pampas grass will rustle there.

LONDON INTERIOR

Autumn is in the air,
The children are playing everywhere.

One dare not open this old door too wide;
It is so dark inside.
The hall smells of dust;
A narrow squirt of sunlight enters high,
Cold, yellow.
The floor creaks, and I hear a sigh,
Rise in the gloom and die.

Through the hall, far away,
I just can see
The dingy garden with its wall and tree.
A yellow cat is sitting on the wall
Blinking toward the leaves that fall.
And now I hear a woman call
Some child from play.

Then all is still. Time must go
Ticking slow, glooming slow.

The evening will turn grey.
It is sad in London after two.
All, all the afternoon
What can old men, old women do?

It is sad in London when the gloom
Thickens, like wool,
In the corners of the room;
The sky is shot with steel,
Shot with blue.

The bells ring the slow time;
The chairs creak, the hours climb;
The sunlight lays a streak upon the floor.

GREAT CITY

When I returned at sunset,
The serving-maid was singing softly
Under the dark stairs, and in the house
Twilight had entered like a moonray.
Time was so dead I could not understand
The meaning of midday or of midnight,
But like falling waters, falling, hissing, falling,
Silence seemed an everlasting sound.

I sat in my dark room,
And watched sunset,
And saw starlight.
I heard the tramp of homing men,
And the last call of the last child;
Then a lone bird twittered,
And suddenly, beyond the housetops,

I imagined dew in the country,
In the hay, on the buttercups,
The rising moon,
The scent of early night,
The songs, the echoes,
Dogs barking,
Day closing,
Gradual slumber,
Sweet rest.

When all the lamps were lighted in the town
I passed into the streetways, and I watched,
Wakeful, almost happy,
And half the night I wandered in the street.

OFFICERS' MESS (1916)

I

I search the room with all my mind,
Peering among those eyes;
For I am feverish to find
A brain with which my brain may talk,
Not that I think myself too wise,
But that I'm lonely, and I walk
Round the large place and wonder – No:
There's nobody, I fear,
Lonely as I, and here.

How they hate me. I'm a fool.
I can't play Bridge; I'm bad at Pool;
I cannot drone a comic song;
I can't talk Shop; I can't use Slang;
My jokes are bad, my stories long:
My voice will falter, break or hang,
Not blurt the sour sarcastic word,
And so my swearing sounds absurd.

II

But came the talk: I found
Three or four others for an argument.
I forced their pace. They shifted their dull ground,
And went
Sprawling about the passages of Thought.
We tugged each other's words until they tore.

They asked me my philosophy: I brought
Bits of it forth and laid them on the floor.
They laughed, and so I kicked the bits about,
Then put them in my pocket one by one,
I, sorry I had brought them out,
They, grateful for the fun.

And when these words had thus been sent
Jerking about, like beetles round a wall,
Then one by one to dismal sleep we went:
There was no happiness at all
In that short hopeless argument
Through yawns and on the way to bed
Among men waiting to be dead.

THE HOPELESS ARGUMENT

I saw two old men sitting by a stove,
Repeating loud illustrious stories
Of blood, and half-forgotten glories.

I said: 'You seem discursive. What of love?'
One said: 'It is a most distressing thing.'
The other, without teeth, began to sing.

So to those old men sitting by that fire,
Trying to warm their hopeless shaking fists,
Dibbing and cuffing their unhappy wrists,

I said: 'Oh, what then of our great desire?'
One cried: 'Desire is certainly no matter.'
The other's crumbling jaws began to chatter.

Then I stared down on them with bitter eyes,
For I was young, and so they wished me dead;
This being wrong, contemptuously I said:

'You are too old for love, but not for lies.'
Shivering, one put on his tattered hat;
The other leant across the fire and spat.

SOLITUDE

When you have tidied all things for the night,
And while your thoughts are fading to their sleep,
You'll pause a moment in the late firelight,
Too sorrowful to weep.

The large and gentle furniture has stood
In sympathetic silence all the day
With that old kindness of domestic wood;
Nevertheless the haunted room will say:
'Some one must be away.'

The little dog rolls over half awake,
Stretches his paws, yawns, looking up at you,
Wags his tail very slightly for your sake,
That you may feel he is unhappy too.

A distant engine whistles, or the floor
Creaks, or the wandering night-wind bangs a door.

Silence is scattered like a broken glass.
The minutes prick their ears and run about,
Then one by one subside again and pass
Sedately in, monotonously out.

You bend your head and wipe away a tear.
Solitude walks one heavy step more near.

ASPIDISTRA STREET

Go along that road, and look at sorrow.
Every window grumbles.
All day long the drizzle fills the puddles,
Trickles in the runnels and the gutters,
Drips and drops and dripples, drops and dribbles,
While the melancholy aspidistra
Frowns between the parlour curtains.

Uniformity, dull Master! –
Birth and marriage, middle-age and death;
Rain and gossip: Sunday, Monday, Tuesday ...

Sure, the lovely fools who made Utopia
Planned it without any aspidistra.
There will be a heaven on earth, but first
We must banish from the parlour
Plush and poker-work and paper flowers,
Brackets, staring photographs and what-nots,
Serviettes, frills and etageres,
Anti-macassars, vases, chiffonniers;

And the gloomy aspidistra
Glowering through the window-pane,
Meditating heavy maxims,
Moralising to the rain.

JOURNEY

I

How many times I nearly miss the train
By running up the staircase once again
For some dear trifle almost left behind.
At that last moment the unwary mind
Forgets the solemn tick of station-time;
That muddy lane the feet must climb –
The bridge – the ticket – signal down –
Train just emerging beyond the town:
The great blue engine panting as it takes
The final curve, and grinding on its brakes
Up to the platform-edge ... The little doors
Swing open, while the burly porter roars.
The tight compartment fills: our careful eyes
Go to explore each others' destinies.
A lull. The station-master waves. The train
Gathers, and grips, and takes the rails again,
Moves to the shining open land, and soon
Begins to tittle-tattle a tame tattoo.

II

They ramble through the country-side,
Dear gentle monsters, and we ride
Pleasantly seated – so we sink
Into a torpor on the brink
Of thought, or read our books, and understand
Half them and half the backward-gliding land:

(Trees in a dance all twirling round;
Large rivers flowing with no sound;
The scattered images of town and field,
Shining flowers half concealed.)
And, having settled to an equal rate,
They swing the curve and straighten to the straight,
Curtail their stride and gather up their joints,
Snort, dwindle their steam for the noisy points,
Leap them in safety, and, the other side,
Loop again to an even stride.

The long train moves: we move in it along.
Like an old ballad, or an endless song,
It drones and wimbles its unwearied croon –
Croons, drones, and mumbles all the afternoon.

Towns with their fifty chimneys close and high,
Wreathed in great smoke between the earth and sky,
It hurtles through them, and you think it must
Halt – but it shrieks and sputters them with dust,
Cracks like a bullet through their big affairs,
Rushes the station-bridge, and disappears
Out to the suburb, laying bare
Each garden trimmed with pitiful care;
Children are caught at idle play,
Held a moment, and thrown away.
Nearly everyone looks round.
Some dignified inhabitant is found
Right in the middle of the commonplace –
Buttoning his trousers, or washing his face.

III

Oh the wild engine! Every time I sit
In any train I must remember it.
The way it smashes through the air; its great
Petulant majesty and terrible rate:
Driving the ground before it, with those round
Feet pounding, beating, covering the ground;
The piston using up the white steam so
You cannot watch it when it come or go;
The cutting, the embankment; how it takes
The tunnels, and the clatter that it makes;
So careful of the train and of the track,
Guiding us out, or helping us go back;
Breasting its destination: at the close
Yawning, and slowly dropping to a doze.

IV

We who have looked each other in the eyes
This journey long, and trundled with the train,
Now to our separate purposes must rise,
Becoming decent strangers once again.
The little chamber we have made our home
In which we so conveniently abode,
The complicated journey we have come,
Must be an unremembered episode.
Our common purpose made us all like friends.
How suddenly it ends!
A nod, a murmur, or a little smile,
Or often nothing, and away we file.

I hate to leave you, comrades. I will stay
To watch you drift apart and pass away.
It seems impossible to go and meet
All those strange eyes of people in the street.
But, like some proud unconscious god, the train
Gathers us up and scatters us again.

from STRANGE MEETINGS

XX

It is not difficult to die:
You hold your breath and go to sleep;
Your skin turns white or grey or blue,
And some of your relations weep.

The cheerful clock without a pause
Will finish your suspended day.
That body you were building up
Will suddenly be thrown away.

You turn your fingers to the ground,
Drop all the things you had to do:
It is the first time in your life
You'll cease completely to be you.

EVENING

Now the cool twilight, glowing,
Falls like dew
Upon the city's brow.
Now fretful day is slowing;
Slowly the river flows, but men are going
Swiftly, as though they knew
At last some hope beyond all silence. Now
To us who wait it seems we had to climb
For this one evening up the hill of Time.

We wait. We wait.
Surely the wings that hold,
Dark-clasped, the mystery of Fate
This moment will unfold.

Now the great hand is lifted that will strike
The final crash on doubt;
The rosy clouds are parted like
Lips that blow some candle out.
The deep breath of the moment is indrawn,
Holds, with wide nostrils, back the final call.
We smile because we know ere dawn
Silence in heavy dust, shall fall.
To-morrow evening all this past will seem
A drifted ancient dream.

Now all the veins of Time are running cool.
Night lies before us like a silent pool.
Oh, at this final moment it is sweet
To go home swiftly through the lighted street.

LOVE IN THE AUTUMN FOREST

She
Let us go back to London. All the trees
Are dying in the forest.

He
Though you fear death.
I thought you would like the colour of the leaves.

She
Let us not remember autumn forests.
Let us forget this falling of the leaves.
In London nothing dies among the streets.

And you will not love me for ever – it is not true.
Say nothing here that is not wholly true;
Or we may hate each other.

Why did we leave the shining pavement;
Pass away from the roaring road?
In London we are known to each other.
But here
Our vows fall like dead leaves.

He
You have slipped your tether.
There, I could well believe you loved the trees;
But here, I see you hate them by your eyes.

Mist clings in your hair.
You stand like a strange martyr.
It hurts you to remain so still.
The leaves are falling in the wood; they are falling;
And life is dumb. We will return.

There, in London we will laugh again.
The tame trees in the square will be enough.
We need not see their leaves fall at our feet.

She
Oh, the autumnal horror covers me.
I wish I could be buried in the leaves.

THE NIGHTINGALE NEAR THE HOUSE

Here is the soundless cypress on the lawn:
It listens, listens. Taller trees beyond
Listen. The moon at the unruffled pond
   Stares. And you sing, you sing.

That star-enchanted song falls through the air
From lawn to lawn down terraces of sound,
Darts in white arrows on the shadowed ground;
   While all the night you sing.

My dreams are flowers to which you are a bee,
As all night long I listen, and my brain
Receives your song, then loses it again
   In moonlight on the lawn.

Now is your voice a marble high and white,
Then like a mist on fields of paradise;
Now is a raging fire, then is like ice,
   Then breaks, and it is dawn.

GOLDFISH

They are the angels of that watery world.
All innocent, they no more than aspire
To move themselves about on golden fins.
Or they can fill their paradise with fire
By darting suddenly from end to end.

Their eyes stare out from far away behind,
And cannot pierce the barrier of Mind.
In the same house are they and we;
Yet well might be
Divided by a whole Eternity.

When twilight flows across the evening room
And air becomes like water, you can feel
Their movements growing larger in the gloom,
And merging with the room, and you are brought
Back where they live, the other side of thought.

Then in the morning, when the seven rays
Of London sunlight one by one incline,
They glide to meet them, and their gulping lips
Suck the light in, so they are caught and played
Like salmon on a heavenly fishing line.

GRAVITY

I

Fit for perpetual worship is the power
That holds our bodies safely to the earth.

When people talk of their domestic gods,
Then privately I think of You.

We ride through space upon your shoulders
Conveniently and lightly set,
And, so accustomed, we relax our hold,
Forget the gentle motion of your body –
But You do not forget.

Sometimes you breathe a little faster,
Or move a muscle:
Then we remember you, O Master.

II

While people meet in reverent groups
And sing to their domestic God,
You, all that time, dear tyrant (How I laugh!)
Could, without effort, place your hand among them,
And sprinkle them.

But all your ways are carefully ordered,
For you have never questioned duty.
We watch your everlasting combinations;

We call them fate; we turn them to our pleasure,
And when they most delight us, call them beauty.

III

I rest my body on your grass,
And let my brain repose in you:
I feel these living moments pass,
And, from within myself to those far places
To be imagined in your time and spaces,
Deliberate the various acts you do: –

Sorting and re-arranging worlds of Matter
Keenly and wisely. Thus you brought our earth
Through stages, and from purpose back to purpose;
From fire to fog, to dust, to birth
Through beast to man, who led himself to brain –
(And you will draw him back to dust again.)

By leave of you he places stone on stone;
He scatters seed: you are at once the prop
Among the long roots of his fragile crop.
You manufacture for him, and insure
House, harvest, implement and furniture,
And hold them all secure.

IV

The hill ... The trees ... From underneath
I feel You pull me with your hand:
Through my firm feet up to my heart

You hold me, – You are in the land,
Reposing underneath the hill.

You keep my balance and my growth.
I lift a foot, but where I go
You follow: you, the ever strong,
Control the smallest thing I do.

If by some little human power
I turn your purpose to my end,
For that I thank you every hour.
I stand at worship, while you send
Thrills up my body to my heart,
And I am all in love to know
How by your strength you keep me part
Of earth, which cannot let me go;
How everything I see around,
Whether it can or cannot move,
Is granted liberty of ground,
And freedom to enjoy your love;

Though you are silent always, and, alone
To You yourself, your power remains unknown.

FATE

I

I have so often
Examined all this well-known room
That I inhabit.

There is the open window;
There the locked door, the door I cannot open,
The only doorway.

When at the keyhole often, often
I bend and listen, I can always hear
A muffled conversation.

An argument:
An angry endless argument of people
Who live behind;

Some loudly talking,
Some dimly into separate conflict moving,
Behind the door.

There they seem prisoned,
As I, in this lone room that I inhabit:
My life; my body.

You, of the previous Being,
You who once made me, and who now discuss me,
Tell me your edict.

You, long ago,
With doubting hands and eager trembling fingers,
Prepared my room.

Before I came,
Each gave a token for remembrance, left it,
And then retired behind the bolted door.

There is the pot of honey
One brought, and there the jar of vinegar
On the same table.

Who poured that water
Shining beside the flask of yellow wine?
Who sighed so softly?

Who brought that living flower to the room?
Who groaned – and I can ever hear the echo?
– You do not answer.

Meanwhile from out the distance
Sounds reach me as of building other houses:
Men building houses.

And if they ever
Should open up a doorway in the wall,
And I pass onward,

What should I take them
Beyond those doorways, in the other rooms?

What shall I bring them,
That they may love me?

Fatal question!
For all the jangling voices rise together:
'What should he take them?'

'What shall he take them?'
Through that locked door there is no final answer.
They are debating, endlessly debating ...

II

O Fate! Have you no other gift
Than voices in a muffled room?
Why do you live behind a door,
And hide yourself in gloom?

And why, again, should you not have
One purpose only, one sole word,
Ringing for ever round my heart:
Plainly delivered, plainly heard?

Your conversation fills my brain
And tortures all my life, and yet
Gives nothing, and I often think
You've grown so old, that you forget;

And having learnt man's fatal trick
Of talking, talking, talking still,
You're tired of definite design,
And laugh at having lost your Will.

THE SILENT POOL

I

I have discovered finally to-day
This home that I have called my own
Is built of straw and clay,
Not, as I thought, of stone.

I wonder who the architect could be,
What builder made it of that stuff;
When it was left to me
The house seemed good enough.

Yet, slowly, as its roof began to sink,
And as its walls began to split,
And I began to think,
Then I suspected it;

But did not clearly know until to-day
That it was only built of straw and clay.

II

Now I will go about on my affairs
As though I had no cares,
Nor ever think at all
How one day soon that house is bound to fall,
So when I'm told the wind has blown it down
I may have something else to call my own.

I have enquired who was the architect,
What builder did erect.
I'm told they did design
Million and million others all like mine,
And argument with all men ends the same: –
It is impossible to fix the blame.

I am so glad that underneath our talk
Our minds together walk.
We argue all the while,
But down below our argument we smile.
We have our houses, but we understand
That our real property is common land.

III

At night we often go
With happy comrades to that real estate,
Where dreams in beauty grow,
And every man enjoys a common fate.

At night in sleep one flows
Below the surface of all argument;
The brain, with all it knows,
Is covered by the waters of content.

But when the dawn appears
Brain rises to the surface with a start,
And, waking, quickly sneers
At the old natural brightness of the heart.

Oh, that a man might choose
To live unconsciously like beast or bird,
And our clear thought not lose
Its beauty when we turn it into word.

IV

Those quarrellings between my brain and heart
(In which I'd take no part)
Pursue their violent course
Corrupting my most vital force
So that my natural property is spent
In fees to keep alive their argument.

V

Look downward in the silent pool:
The weeds cling to the ground they love;
They live so quietly, are so cool;
They do not need to think, or move.

Look down in the unconscious mind:
There everything is quiet too
And deep and cool, and you will find
Calm growth and nothing hard to do,
And nothing that need trouble you.

FRAGMENT

Who talked of God? Who talked of peace?
  Or the great next Great War to come?
Who talked of times when war shall cease,
  And men walk slowly home?

I heard a jabbering mass of tongues
  Expending words on brilliant air;
Through flashing lips I heard great lungs
  Proclaiming courage mighty fair.

Gigantic vanities low sprang
  And captured by the flimsy hair
That innocence whose quick cries rang
  To nowhere through enormous air.

The Vast Directors growled and spumed,
  The sirens from the Factories shrieked,
And all the Earth was vaguely fumed
  Drenched with calm smoke, and coned, and streaked.

I held my hands back to my heart
  And watched like someone at a show
Who waits dispassionately apart
  For what the unknown dice may throw.

Then suddenly from out my dreams
  A great God furiously appeared.

'The World is not,' he said, 'what seems;
'This World is not what you have feared.'

Then cosily I settled down,
   Thinking: An idle dream I've had,
Yet all my body waxed in frown;
   Are dreams so mad? Are dreams so mad?

    . . . . .

I spring to life from out the dark.
   Is new illumination sent?
Some God is – if all men could hark –
   Through private vision vaguely blent.

He will not visit me to-night,
   To-morrow, or another day;
But He, thank Him, will re-appear
   In all I do, or think, or say.

I'm stupid, yet I'm better far
   Than He, and He will never know
This all consuming avatar
   In which I am, and live, and grow.

    . . . . . .

I'm worried, God, by your pale voice.
   You are unlike us. We to-day
In our own anxious flesh rejoice,
   Deaf to whatever you can say.

Ring your old thunder: we won't hear.
   String lightning: we have got that down.
It is no good if you draw near.
   We're settled in our final town.

No wireless you can now contrive,
   Old Patriarch, will make us seem
More than we are, that is, alive,
   Dependent on an anxious dream.

SAFE PASSAGE

The stream of traffic flowed along the street.
We waited at the corner – whom to meet?
In this gigantic town, plain life should be
Simpler than most remote simplicity –
But in the turmoil of this unreal town
With parched hard tongue and face turned dustward down
One lies and tries to hold one's gulp of breath
Fighting so feebly against calm death.

I would so like Life to die, if only
One did not think too much of being lonely,
And of the large and angry forms that rise
All night in dreams and fill their hopeless skies.

TO THE LADIES OF THE CONVENT

They do exist; for I have seen their House.
An ugly structure, gothic-windowed, hard,
Pale, gaunt and plain, brick-built, with slated roof,
Surrounded by thin brick-builded wall,
Enclosed discreetly by a lean old hedge of
Rustling yews that meditate on dust.

Who are they, who, within, not ever seen,
Commune upon the silence of their God?
He will not speak; nor ever spoke to-day.
Their floating Prayer has become a kind
Of vague enticement to an absent love.

But as I pass this Convent I can't help
Dreaming about their virgin thought of Him.
If they should come outside into the world,
Maybe he would be wandering down the Strand,
Or strolling into Piccadilly Circus.

O, chimèd, secret, formal discipline!
Forgive me that I pause and gently laugh.
Great oceans of the breaking buttercup
Yellow, incestuous, without any care
Are foaming over pasture to your wall.

You can't defeat this imminent attack,
Summer is raging through the frantic country;
Thorn, may, and elder breed gigantic hedgerows

Sprouting across indefinite wild limits,
Spreading themselves like fools and never asking:
Lilac; laburnum: with their sudden ending,
Great, large and terrible, like something doomed.

I know the cold delight you have upon you.
You give so little, but receive for ever.
Conscience is like a policeman in your cells.

It would be strange if you could lie among them,
Press your chilled temples closely to their bodies.
Be like an everlasting understanding,
Be like the God you have so blindly worshipped,
Be like a buttercup, a mustard seed,
Or field of pasture: How the silk would rustle.
Black-robes, give up your bodies for a moment.

But the tall bricks that wall you are too safe.
The yews, the cypresses, the crucifix.
You will remain upon your virgin beds
Dreaming of sweet Communion holy bright,
Harmless, and comfortably always right,
Sure there is harm in night, which you are: Night.

DISILLUSIONMENT

When all our words have gone too far
   And cannot well retract;
While all the deeds we swore we'd do
   Are flowing into act.
Then we will pick our bodies up
   Deliberately try
But on the point of trying best
   We bend ourselves and die.

So when you ramble making all
   The promises you must,
Remember that your pledge is but
   From dust and unto dust,
And every brave delightful oath
   You make for being true
Is mortgaged and disqualified
   By coming out of you.

You speak because a little thought
   Is rambling through your brain,
And, on the verge of death, you fear
   You may not talk again.
Oh, large delightful power of speech
   I'm tired because of you:
Oh, wild ideal of swearing well
   What you can never do.

I'll go away this very night
   And leave my comrades here
And never talk to them again
   Who trust me and are dear.
We who have passed the ancient state
   Of speculating brain
We'll drink a glass and part and pass
   And never hope again.

CROSSING A BRIDGE

That bridge has never yet been measured;
It is more long than any bridge before.
Daylong, nightlong, yearlong, nightmare-long
There is a crossing of it, and a roar
Of oily-livered engines which to feed
Ten million tanks drip their explosive fumes
Threading a vibrant romp of speed.
Crossing a bridge; crossing a bridge: that's all.

They are not sure of what they have to do
Except they know that they must stamp their way
Through time, leave time behind them, beat the day,
Leave it behind, leave everything; go, go
Forward, away, grind, screw, drive, thrash, compel,
Cleave, grapple, shoot toward the other end.
There rings; there rings an everlasting bell:

A summons; an alarm; a drive; a call,
A cry beyond an iron unopened door;
Or knuckles flapping on a hollow wall;
Or in a cage, a roar;
Or in a desert no escape to hills;
Or in a valley, longing for the sea:
A strangled rush of overmastered wills
Imagining a chance of being free.

IN THE NIGHT

Over my head
The hard cool face of grief stares all the night.
My hateful bed
Is never silent, creaking every time I move.
I am tortured, fevered with the poison of love
All crumpled waiting for my love's delight.

The stupid hours die and then live again
Winding their cogged and ticking flight of pain.
Morning will come at last I fear, I know.
Strike the foul vengeful gong when I must rise
Patiently, quickly through the tired day go,
Curse my dear love and swallow its loud cries.

Where is your face you torturer, what are your hands
Doing so far away from eager mine?
I hope you may be sad in other lands
Tired, cold and suffering. Then my body flies
Voyaging to comfort you and intertwine
Its longing with your fate and with your sighs

But are you dead? Then I become a ghost
Hovering and haunting like a bird of prey
Crying above you, I will dare the boast
I could pick out your soul and soar away
Into the night and bring you – you shall lie
In vain dead. I still love though you may die.

The face of grief floats through the haunted room
And covers all the furniture. Hard time
Will you not crack and flood about the gloom?
O, I am tired of this abortive rime
It does not bring you back friend far away –
Light claws between the curtains. – It is day.

THE CURATE'S CHRISTMAS EVE

The Curate and the Spinster sit,
   (O gentle dear timidity!)
Her yearning thought, his untried wit,
   Her aspidistra and their tea
Combine to make their Christmas Eve complete
Within itself; and neither sour nor sweet.

Why should the moralist complain?
   The sentimentalist deride?
She turns fond eyes on him in vain:
   She will not ever be a bride,
For he is doomed to pass eternity
Sipping, O, nothing more than, sipping tea.

She will not be compelled to scold,
   Nor he be driven to complain.
They are better both than any gold.
   No mistletoe, and no champagne,
Will make her less a maid, him more a priest,
Or turn their Christian to a pagan feast.

UNANSWERED QUESTION

Shall you and I leave everything behind,
Go westward walking,
Never again be conscious of the mind,
But walking, talking
Of flowers and birds and clouds, with no routine,
Not wonder ever again what consciousness may mean?

Shall you and I go eastward in grave thought
And inward prying,
Be conscious, introspective, haggard, caught
Sighing and whying;
With all clear mind and valuable breath
Expended on cold doubts about eventual death?

Will you and I, submitting to the wind,
Go northward roaring?
That may be one good way to leave behind
The too trim harbour mooring:
Partake some great campaign, some large experience, some
Worthy extensive excuse for returning glorious home.

Can you and I go southward without blame
Into the region we love,
Fading without desire for famous name,
Or calculated move?
Can we in sunlight, both contentedly,
Live without ambition, gazing at blue sea?

THE TERRIBLE DOOR

Too long outside your door I have shivered.
You open it? I will not stay.
I'm haunted by your ashen beauty.
Take back your hand. I have gone away.

Don't talk, but move to that near corner.
I loathe the long cold shadow here.
We will stand a moment in the lamplight,
Until I watch you hard and near.

Happy release! Good-bye for ever!
Here at the corner we say good-bye.
But if you want me, if you do need me,
Who waits, at the terrible door, but I?

RUMOUR

Somebody is whispering on the stair.
What are those words half spoken, half drawn back?
Whence are those muffled words, some red, some black?
Who is whispering? Who is there?

Somebody is sneaking up the stair,
His feet approaching every doorway,
Yet never a moment standing anywhere.

Now many whisper close outside some door.
O suddenly push it open wide.
You see: whoever said he heard them, he has lied.

And yet words are left dark like heavy dust
In many rooms, or red on iron like rust:
And who contrives to leave them? Some one must.

In every street, this noisy town of ours
Has stealthy whispering watchers walking round,
Recording all our movements, every sound,
Hissing and shuffling, and they may have found
To-day my name: to-morrow they'll find yours.

TOO NEAR THE SEA

No foam;
A trippling shallow tread;
The pebbles tingle on the beach,
While, disentangled over head
From clouds, the moonlight, carefully spread,
Lays whiter sheets on my white bed.

From haunted sleeplessness, in quivering dread,
I wander through the sea-sound-empty-full
Large sleeping room above that sea. My bed
Felt like a raft; but now there is the pull
Of dreary sea, toward the window drawing,
Of every slight wave with its itch and drag
Upward toward the tall lean windows clawing,
And, sea-bemysteried, my senses flag.
Yesterday and to-morrow will be waves
Breaking in calm succession on to-day.
Earth-life pales down to sea-foam. Flesh behaves
Like sifted ashes.
Cold slow ocean washes
All round, and then it washes me away.

THE OCEAN IN LONDON

In London while I slowly wake
At morning I'm amazed to hear
The ocean, seventy miles away,
Below my window roaring, near.

When first I know that heavy sound
I keep my eyelids closely down,
And sniff the brine, and hold all thought
Reined back outside the walls of town.

So I can hardly well believe
That those tremendous billows are
Of iron and steel and wood and glass:
Van, lorry, and gigantic car.

MIDNIGHT LAMENTATION

When you and I go down
Breathless and cold,
Our faces both worn back
To earthly mould,
How lonely we shall be!
What shall we do,
You without me,
I without you?

I cannot bear the thought
You, first, may die,
Nor of how you will weep,
Should I.
We are too much alone;
What can we do
To make our bodies one:
You, me; I, you?

We are most nearly born
Of one same kind;
We have the same delight,
The same true mind.
Must we then part, we part;
Is there no way
To keep a beating heart,
And light of day?

I could now rise and run
Through street on street
To where you are breathing – you,
That we might meet,
And that your living voice
Might sound above
Fear, and we two rejoice
Within our love.

How frail the body is,
And we are made
As only in decay
To lean and fade.
I think too much of death;
There is a gloom
When I can't hear your breath
Calm in some room.

O, but how suddenly
Either may droop;
Countenance be so white,
Body stoop.
Then there may be a place
Where fading flowers
Drop on a lifeless face
Through weeping hours.

Is then nothing safe?
Can we not find
Some everlasting life

In our one mind?
I feel it like disgrace
Only to understand
Your spirit through your word,
Or by your hand.

I cannot find a way
Through love and through;
I cannot reach beyond
Body, to you.
When you or I must go
Down evermore,
There'll be no more to say
– But a locked door.

WHERE SHE LIVES

We love the room; and it is ours;
But when I came to you to-day,
You were possessed by other powers:
You spoke, but you were far away.

I saw you pale against the wall,
Half hidden in a shaft of light.
I thought I heard a petal fall,
Yet disbelieved both sound and sight.

The traffic on the street roared by:
I trembled in the room alone.
I heard you move, then heard you sigh;
Yet wondered: Is she here, or gone?

Your lips were moved, yet, one by one,
Your words like dropping petals fell.
I whispered: surely, she is gone;
Cried inwardly: I cannot tell.

Room, come to life! Shine phantom wall!
Light, light, become you calm, and keen!
The shadows tremble, and are tall,
And everything is dimly seen.

Put your cold hands, and may they fall,
Loose, gently, on my tortured mind.
Room, come to life: shine phantom wall.

GREAT DISTANCE

How can you be so far away?
When I have been in pain before
I've found you standing just outside
My body's door,
In patient silence waiting there,
That I might feel your spirit near.

But now, with every breath I take,
It seems that you are farther gone,
And I become more wide awake,
And more alone.
In all this world there is no light;
No open doorway here to-night.

I lay my body on the bed,
And cross my arms, and think of death,
And think, nine hundred miles away,
You draw calm breath.
At last, imagination through
That distance reaches out to you.

Now you are leaning on your hand,
And staring at an empty book.
You raise your eyes; you understand:
I feel your look
Pierce through me. In this foreign place
You reach me, and I know your face.

I swear that then our hands did touch,
And all my fainting pain is gone;
I know that you did touch my hand.
Each is alone.
Yet loneliness begins to seem
Like sleep, and will become a dream.

SILENCE BETWEEN

Does not my ghost appear?
My eyes feel over intervening space,
   And I am leaning forward at the strain
Till, now, my fingers nearly touch your face.
   Lean out to me: I'm calling with my brain.

Do you not feel me near?
I'm bending forward on the wind of thought,
   Sailing toward you on the lake of mind.
O share this moment which may not be brought
   Ever to life again, once left behind.

But I can only hear
Far off the beating of your lonely heart,
   While in between us flow the hurrying waves.
A deathly wind is blowing us apart:
   Lovers are not more foreign in their graves.

NEW DAY

And how will fancy lead his life to-day?
Eyes lift their shutters. Still the room is grey.
But slowly it reveals (with blankets back)
Omens all clothed in blue; or green; or black.
How will the small things of the day behave?
Will hope be calm, or petulantly rave?

There'll be no great decision. Time will knit,
And multiply the stitches while we look.
A few hours we shall stand, a few hours sit,
A few hours talk, or walk, or read a book.
The dishes will be washed, the table laid.
Smells of sweet food will spread delicious wings.
The daily commonplaces will be said,
And we shall handle all the daily things.

And so the time will pass.
Yet is there not a meaning in our looks
That makes us kindred as the blades of grass,
Or tree-leaves leaning over country brooks?
May we not be aware somehow
Among the cool small habits we have made
Of calm hands or a sympathetic brow,
Or of a guiding motive in the shade?

Yes! Yes! Oh what delusion have I had? –
Only to-day discovered you?
No wonder yesterday remained so sad.

Let us find out what Love intends to do.
Meanwhile for me
The moments will be only two or three.
Some little glance of yours will send me mad;
Some other look of yours will set me free;
Some word you drop make my whole body sad.
Some thing you do will send my spirit flying
Into the blue of wild delight;
And next the thought of you will leave my body lying
In passionate waking dreams all through to-night.

UNTO HER

O, flower of my life, I bring my heart
To you, and find you waking with a start.

The bed is made, and you, half smile, half frown;
Have been a tedious two hours lying down.

Have dozed and wakened, dozed and waked again,
Imagined joy, felt everlasting pain.

I come, I come; I bring, I bring my grief,
That burns my dismal soul without relief.

But your slim arms receive me in their fold,
You warm my heart. My body that was cold

Receives your lifefull gift, and now I find
Peace and eventual Heaven in your mind;

And in your body, that one place I have sought,
A tranquil lodging for my stormy thought.

THE ONE, FAITHFUL

How many words may pass
Before one ever makes a friend
And all that conversation prove, alas,
However subtle, nothing in the end.

Searching I found and thought, 'I will enrol
You slowly, peacefully among those of mine
Who can pass out beyond the initial toll
Of comradeship through necessary wine.'

But, probing, I discovered, with what pain,
Wine more essential in the end than you,
And boon-companionship left me again
Less than I had been, with no more to do
Than drop pale hands towards their hips and keep
Friendship for speculation or for sleep.

We persons multiplied upon this earth
Meet hardly ever, or when we have found
Each other built congenial by our birth
Then we, just then, suspect the common ground
The voice, the way, the manner and the sound.

Friendship may be too difficult to win –
May end too quickly in a faint distrust,
Or may be found too sharply to begin
In its mere finding, a disgust.

So shall I turn to you my only friend
And going to you find you always there?
(I thought that) I return to you. I bend
My lips towards your eyes for what I miss
But just as we are sloping toward our kiss
I feel them moistened by your lonely tear.

BITTER SANCTUARY

I

She lives in the porter's room; the plush is nicotined.
Clients have left their photos there to perish.
She watches through green shutters those who press
To reach unconsciousness.

She licks her varnished thin magenta lips,
She picks her foretooth with a finger nail,
She pokes her head out to greet new clients, or
To leave them (to what torture) waiting at the door.

II

Heat has locked the heavy earth,
Given strength to every sound,
He, where his life still holds him to the ground,
In anæsthesia, groaning for re-birth,
Leans at the door.
From out the house there comes the dullest flutter;
A lackey; and thin giggling from behind that shutter.

III

His lost eyes lean to find and read the number.
Follows his knuckled rap, and hesitating curse.
He cannot wake himself; he may not slumber;
While on the long white wall across the road
Drives the thin outline of a dwindling hearse.

IV

Now the door opens wide.
He: 'Is there room inside?'
She: 'Are you past the bounds of pain?'
He: 'May my body lie in vain
    Among the dreams I cannot keep!'
She: 'Let him drink the cup of sleep.'

V

Thin arms and ghostly hands; faint sky-blue eyes;
Long drooping lashes, lids like full-blown moons,
Clinging to any brink of floating skies:
What hope is there? What fear? – Unless to wake and see
Lingering flesh, or cold eternity.

O yet some face, half living, brings
Far gaze to him and croons:
She: 'You're white. You are alone.
    Can you not approach my sphere?'
He: 'I'm changing into stone.'
She: 'Would I were! Would *I* were!'
Then the white attendants fill the cup.

VI

In the morning through the world,
Watch the flunkeys bring the coffee;
Watch the shepherds on the downs,
Lords and ladies at their toilet,
Farmers, merchants, frothing towns.

But look how he, unfortunate, now fumbles
Through unknown chambers, unheedful stumbles.
Can he evade the overshadowing night?
Are there not somewhere chinks of braided light?

VII

How do they leave who once are in those rooms?
Some may be found, they say, deeply asleep
In ruined tombs.
Some in white beds, with faces round them. Some
Wander the world, and never find a home.

BIBLIOGRAPHY

There are, as far as I can discover, no books in print by Harold Monro and no books in print directly concerned with his work and his life. A few of his poems are scattered in anthologies, but in such a way that they make little impression. The books I am listing here need to be supplemented by exploring the internet for information about Monro, but there is enough of his work in my selection to allow readers to make up their own minds as to its value. So, here is an essential list, although all or most of these books are out of print:

The Collected Poems of Harold Monro, edited by Alida Monro, with a biographical sketch by F.S. Flint and a critical note by T.S. Eliot (Cobden-Sanderson, 1933)

Twentieth Century Poetry, an anthology chosen by Harold Monro (Chatto and Windus, 1920)

Some Contemporary Poets, Harold Monro (Leonard Parsons, 1920; Simpkin Marshall, 1928)

Harold Monro and the Poetry Bookshop, Joy Grant (Routledge and Kegan Paul, 1967)

Georgian Poetry 1911-1922, edited by Timothy Rogers. Critical

Heritage series. (Routledge, 1977. Reprinted, 1997)
A Map of Modern English Verse, John Press (OUP, 1969)
Life for Life's Sake, Richard Aldington (Cassell, 1968)
Ushant, Conrad Aiken (New York, 1952)

There are useful critical views of Monro, all of which are sympathetic, in:

English Poetry 1900-1950, C.H. Sisson (Carcanet, 1981)
Guide to Modern World Literature, Volume 1, Martin Seymour-Smith (Hodder and Stoughton, 1985)
Who's Who in Twentieth Century Literature, Martin Seymour-Smith (Weidenfeld and Nicholson, 1976.)

Those who wish to study the subject in greater depth, need access to a good university library, where the following sources might be found:

'Coming to London', Geoffrey Grigson (*London Magazine*, June 1956)
'A Letter from London', Amy Lowell (*Little Review*, September 1914)
'The Poetry Bookshop', Amy Lowell (*Little Review*, May 1915)
'Reflections on Contemporary Poetry', T.S. Eliot (*Egoist*, September 1917)
'Prolegomena to Poetry', T.S. Eliot (*Dial*, April 1921)
'Harold Monro, Literary Midwife' (*Arizona Quarterly*, Winter 1949)
'Nerve Emotions', Harriet Monroe (*Poetry*, August 1930)
'Harold Monro', Harriet Monroe (*Poetry*, May 1932)
'Harold Monro', Ezra Pound (*Criterion*, July 1932)
'Harold Monro: A Study in Integration', D.S. Savage (*Poetry*, September 1942)

By far the very best introduction, both to his life and his poetry, is *Harold Monro and the Poetry Bookshop* by Joy Grant, listed above. Without this I would have been unable to write the introduction to this book. Any serious student of Harold Monro should make every effort to obtain a secondhand copy.

GREENWICH EXCHANGE
SELECTED POETRY LIST

Gary ALLEN
Jackson's Corner
£11.99 (pbk) ♦ 94pp ♦ 2016
978-1-910996-03-4

Joseph ALLEN
Clabber Street Blues
£11.99 (pbk) ♦ 88pp ♦ 2016
978-1-910996-07-2

Charles BAUDELAIRE
Les Fleurs du Mal (edited F.W. Leakey)
£9.95 (pbk) ♦ 160pp ♦ 1997
978-1-871551-10-5

Maggie BUTT
Lipstick
£7.99 (pbk) ♦ 72pp ♦ 2007
978-1-871551-94-5

Michael CULLUP
A Change of Season
£9.95 (pbk) ♦ 98pp ♦ 2010
978-1-906075-38-5

Michael CULLUP
Matelot
£11.99 (pbk) ♦ 132pp ♦ 2016
978-1-906075-95-8

Simon DAVID
a rainbow of only one hue
£11.95 (pbk) ♦ 96pp ♦ 2016
978-1-910996-99-7

John GREENING
Hunts: Poems 1979-2009
£7.99 (pbk) ♦ 262 pp ♦ 2009
978-1-906075-33-0

Sean HALDANE
The Memory Tree
£9.99 (pbk) ♦ 90pp ♦ 2015
978-1-906075-94-1

Sean HALDANE
Always Two: Poems 1966-2009
£15.99 (pbk) ♦ 268pp ♦ 2009
978-1-906075-22-4

Ralph HODGSON
The Last Blackbird & Other Poems
£7.95 (pbk) ♦ 68pp ♦ 2004
978-1-871551-81-5

Warren HOPE
First Light & Other Poems
£9.99 (pbk) ♦ 60pp ♦ 2013
978-1-906075-80-4

Warren HOPE
Adam's Thoughts in Winter
£4.99 (pbk) ♦ 46pp ♦ 2001
978-1-871551-40-2

Gordon JARVIE
A Man Passing Through
£16.99 (pbk) ♦ 252pp ♦ 2014
978-1-906075-89-7

Gordon JARVIE
Endgame
£11.99 (pbk) ♦ 80pp ♦ 2016
978-1-910996-98-0

John LUCAS
Portable Property
£9.99 (pbk) ♦ 82pp ♦ 2015
978-1-910996-00-3

Hollie MCNISH
Papers
£11.95 (pbk) ♦ 76pp ♦ 2012
978-1-906075-67-5

Derwent MAY
Wondering About Many Women
£7.99 (pbk) ♦ 46pp ♦ 2011
978-1-906075-62-0

Robert NYE
An Almost Dancer
£7.99 (pbk) ♦ 58pp ♦ 2012
978-1-906075-39-2

Robert NYE
The Rain and the Glass
£6.99 (pbk) ♦ 132pp ♦ 2004
978-1-871551-41-9

Steven O'BRIEN
Scrying Stone
£7.99 (pbk) ♦ 70pp ♦ 2010
978-1-906075-56-9

Marnie POMEROY
Blue Moon
£9.99 (pbk) ♦ 76pp ♦ 2015
978-1-910996-02-7

Marnie POMEROY
The Flaming
£7.99 (pbk) ♦ 80pp ♦ 2010
978-1-906075-43-9

Martin SEYMOUR-SMITH
Collected Poems 1943-1993
£9.99 (pbk) ♦ 184pp ♦ 2006
978-1-871551-47-1

Martin SEYMOUR-SMITH
Wilderness
£4.99 (pbk) ♦ 52pp ♦ 1994
978-1-871551-08-2

David SUTTON
No Through Road
£9.99 (pbk) ♦ 48pp ♦ 2013
978-1-906075-77-4

Jim C. WILSON
Come Close and Listen
£9.99 (pbk) ♦ 88pp ♦ 2014
978-1-906075-85-9

Stephen WILSON
Fluttering Hands
£7.95 (pbk) ♦ 80pp ♦ 2008
978-1-906075-19-4